DRACONIAN GOETIA

GOETIA IN THE QLIPHOTH SYSTEM

A.C. MONT

DRACONIAN GOETIA

GOETIA IN THE QLIPHOTH SYSTEM

2023

Draconian Goetia: goetia in the qliphoth system
© 2023, A.C. Mont

Editing ▲ Sitra Ahra Publications

Book design ▲ Sitra Ahra Publications

Cover artwork ▲ A.C. Mont

Illustrations ▲ A.C. Mont

M757g
   Mont, A.C.
      Draconian goetia: goetia in the qliphoth system / A.C.
   Mont. – Sitra Ahra Publications, 2023.
   Includes bibliographical references.

   ISBN: 978-65-994933-6-2
   1. Psychology. 2. Occult philosophy. 3. Goetia. I. Title. II.
   Mont, A.C.

Sitra Ahra ▲ sitraahra11@gmail.com

TABLE OF CONTENTS

INTRODUCTION 7

TOOLS 9

GOETIC ENTITIES 15

IAO OPERATION 89

GOETIA OPERATION (Active practice) 93

GOETIA OPERATION (Semi-passive practice) 97

Appendix 1 – Hours table 101

Appendix 2 – Hours calculation 102

Appendix 3 – Glossary 103

Bibliography 105

INTRODUCTION

▲ "Goetia" comes from the Greek word *goeteia*, which means "sorcery". In the beginning, it was the somber practice of mourning the deceased in funeral rites and, later, of trying to contact the dead in order to obtain knowledge. From that context, goetia was developed as a means of contacting the "dead" chthonic entities, that is, entities from the underworld, from the depths of caves and grottoes on Earth, or from the "world of the dead". Since its early Greek beginnings, goetia seems to have been an individual practice, of personal experience, even reaching its excessive medievalesque ecclesiastical form as a monotheistic pseudepigraphical document that described entities of pagan mythological polytheism (or supposedly "strange" entities, of the people not converted to monotheism).

Here, in this work, goetia is presented in conformity with the draconian qabalah structure (qliphoth planetary system), according to the entities-codes pertinent attributions, such as: attainment, psychoaromata (incense and essential oil), operation hours, names pronunciation, keys-sigils colours (seals), and more.

Using a direct, clear and objective language, without vague or obscure terms, without stagnant medievalisms, and, by extension, without old-fashioned nobiliary and monarchical vocabulary, goetia is brought to a more current and facilitated understanding, so that its study and practice are accessible, without unnecessary excesses and no ecclesiastical dogmas.

TOOLS

▲ The entire system of draconian goetia has its specific features: keys-sigils colours, tools, celestial objects attributions, operation hours, names pronunciation, etc. Therefore, the goetic operator must try to follow the instructions for preparing the tools and devices described here.

BOMOS

A trunk-table used as a "basis" for neuropsychic processes (acts ritualized systems for working with the neuropsyche), as a starting and turning point, serving as a support for other tools, instruments, and materials. It should preferably be made of wood, with the appearance of a black double cube of 1 metre height, 50 centimetres width, 50 centimetres lenght – or half the height of the person (the goetic operator). If the bomos is not possible, a suitable table or counter can be used.

Bomos

ROBE

The vestment that serves to assist the operator in the neuropsychic convention of mental and emotional isolation from external interference, facilitating the inner recollection, the mental concentration, and the access to the goetic neuropsychic levels. It may be a comfortable black hooded robe made of natural fibers, and it may be girded at the waist with cincture (cord), in the appropriate basic colour, or simply an all-purpose white cincture. If the robe is not possible, some clean black cloth can be used.

BELL

A brass hand bell used to create a favourable mental and emotional "atmosphere", signaling the opening and closing of the operations, marking the operations stages, and "awakening" the operator from the goetic neuropsychic process.

Bell

WAND

A rod or stick used, in general, for the neuropsychic conventions of goetic forces activation and direction in ritualistic operations. It may be made manually of straight and smooth wood, the bark subsequently removed, the length of the forearm of the operator. It may have a symmetrical colourless rock crystal at the top end and a copper wire connected to it that traverses the entire length of the wood. Alternatively, you can purchase a radiesthesia wand or a crystal-tipped stick, both commercially available.

Radiesthesia wand

INCENSE BURNER

A censer or an incense burner to smoke the place of operations and favour goetic activities. In use, it may compose an atmosphere to predispose the individual's neuropsychic perception levels. It may be a common incense burner, for good quality natural psychoaromatic incense sticks.

PSYCHOAROMATAS

The substances for smoking (incense) of the operations place and tools, to be placed on the bomos and into the goetic triangle, and for anointing (essential oils) – three drops of oil onto the feet, wrists, nape of the neck, temples, and centre of the forehead (take an allergy test first).

CANDLES and LAMPS

The tools used to illuminate the bomos and the operations place. They also serve to provide the "atmosphere" and assist the operator in the mental convention of connection with the specific goetic forces. One of the lamps may be installed on the ceiling, just above the bomos; another, in the appropriate basic colour, may be located in the triangle. The candles, in candlesticks, may be in the appropriate basic colours, optionally greased with the appropriate essential oil (psychoaromata), one candle on the bomos and the other in the triangle.

CIRCLE

A graphic device used to delimit the operational area and encompass the operador in the personal dimension, for the individual to concentrate mental and emotional energy, making the neuropsychic conventions and psychomental deimpregnation before operations to eliminate undesirable mental and emotional elements. The circle can be drawn on the ground with charcoal or chalk and sea salt, in a size that can fit the operator, the bomos, and other objects.

TRIANGLE

Graphic device used to delimit the physical-intellectual "place", being the focus of goetic projections, or activated neuropsychic manifestations. The base of this equilateral triangle can be 60 centimetres, and must be located 60 centimetres outside the circle, with the apex facing the north quadrant (cardinal point). In the centre, the goetic key-sigil in the appropriate colours should be placed.

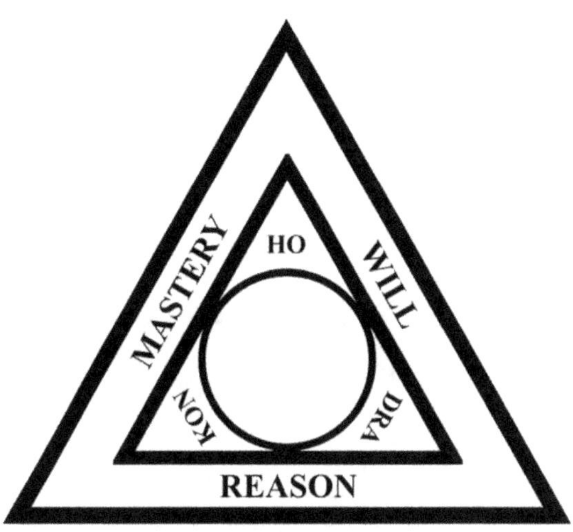

KEYS-SIGILS

The graphic devices that must be hand-painted in the appropriate pantacular colours or digitally colourized and then printed in vivid colours on hard paper, thus composing pantacular seals. Note: "pantacular" comes from the word "pantacle", not "pentacle" (see the glossary for the difference).

GOETIC ENTITIES

▲ The goetic forces, or "dead" entities of the deep (parts of the neuropsychic system not yet activated, apparently "dead", or "hidden" by the superficial neuropsyche, the default mode network), due to their attributions and features, transit in the mental and emotional levels of the qliphoth planetary system – the deep neuropsyche (the "nightside", the "hidden"). From these levels (or "shells"), in which they are contained, the forces can be brought "closer" to the material level, where the neuropsyche externalized attainments and the internalized neuropsychic manifestations of the physical individual take place. Aspects of the mental and emotional levels are here expressed by the entities-codes with their archetypal names and symbols. These symbols, or keys-sigils, along with the names, have the function of "awakening", or activating, the mental and emotional aspects so that they manifest internally or externally, under control and direction, through changes in the neuropsychic system (which occur due to the active and semi-passive goetic operations). The operations to activate the forces of such neuropsychic levels, through each goetic entity-code, are personal and individual, as specific thoughts and intense emotions must be involved, in order to astralize (charge with energy) the keys-sigils and the names, helping the operator in the possible attainments. All that with strong will, rational control, conscious decision, concentrated attention, and defined objectives.

BAEL

1

▲ Qliphotic Solarian force in the mental and emotional levels of the neuropsyche, which is to be manifested and controlled; levels identified with the entity-code Bael.

- **Attainments:** capacity for authority; conscious self-criticism; development of the sense of self; capacity for discretion and prudence; wisdom to decide for social distance when necessary; capacity for solitude and tranquility; insight discernment in the chaotic creative processes of the mind; conscious and deliberate effort to achieve clear goals or defined objectives.
- **Qabalistic qlipha:** Thagiriron – the "shell" of Solarian forces; name pronounced clearly, gutturally, and quickly.
- **Operation hours:** 3rd and 10th night hours of Sunday. (See *Appendix 1 – Hours table* and *Appendix 2 – Hours calculation*)
- **Psychoaromata:** spikenard.
- **Name pronunciation:** name Bael, guttural and fast.
- **Pantacular colours:** key-sigil in violet on yellow background.
- **Basic colour:** yellow.
- **Sound frequencies:** E music note (330 Hz) and A-sharp music note (466 Hz) sounding together.

AGARES

2

▲ Qliphotic Mercurian force in the mental and emotional levels of the neuropsyche, which is to be manifested and controlled; levels identified with the entity-code Agares.

- **Attainments:** skills in communication; capacity for language systems learning; sense of cunning and guile; great perception of other people's intentions beyond appearances; skills for deceit and scam; ability to cause shame, infamy, and humiliation to others; search and seizure ability; psychic adaptation to space-time.
- **Qabalistic qlipha:** Samael – the "shell" of Mercurian forces; name pronounced clearly, hoarsely, and with a hissing S.
- **Operation hours:** 3rd and 10th night hours of Wednesday. (See *Appendix 1 – Hours table* and *Appendix 2 – Hours calculation*)
- **Psychoaromata:** storax (benzoin).
- **Name pronunciation:** name Agares, clearly, hoarsely, with a hissing S.
- **Pantacular colours:** key-sigil in blue on orange background.
- **Basic colour:** orange.
- **Sound frequencies:** G music note (392 Hz) and C-sharp music note (554 Hz) sounding together.

VASSAGO

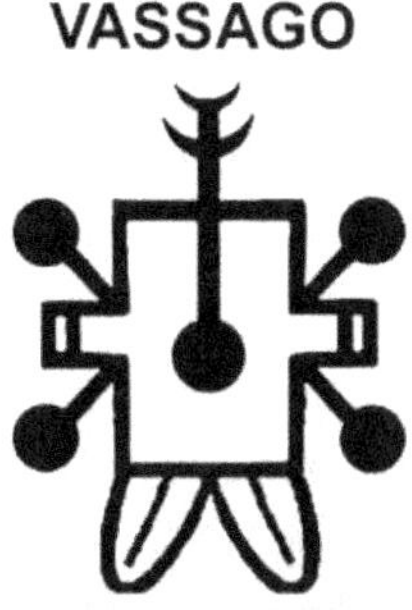

3

▲ Qliphotic Solarian force in the mental and emotional levels of the neuropsyche, which is to be manifested and controlled; levels identified with the entity-code Vassago.

- **Attainments:** self-discovery; knowledge of things once hidden; ability to recover memories; knowledge of the past and preparation for the future; ability to anticipate events; capacity for self-defense and protection against intellectual attacks, emotional blackmail, and mind games; ability to give persuasive and attractive speeches.
- **Qabalistic qlipha:** Thagiriron – the "shell" of Solarian forces; name pronounced clearly, gutturally, and quickly.
- **Operation hours:** 3rd and 10th night hours of Sunday. (See *Appendix 1 – Hours table* and *Appendix 2 – Hours calculation*)
- **Psychoaromata:** spikenard.
- **Name pronunciation:** name Vassago, guttural and fast.
- **Pantacular colours:** key-sigil in violet on yellow background.
- **Basic colour:** yellow.
- **Sound frequencies:** E music note (330 Hz) and A-sharp music note (466 Hz) sounding together.

SAMIGINA

4

▲ Qliphotic Mercurian force in the mental and emotional levels of the neuropsyche, which is to be manifested and controlled; levels identified with the entity-code Samigina.

- **Attainments:** ability to subvert and transgress through words (written or spoken); control of information and knowledge; amoral or subversive knowledge acquisition; capacity to identify common sense; capacity to learn about liberal arts and sciences (arithmetic, geometry, astronomy, music; grammar, logic, rhetoric); ability to guide and comfort those who have lost someone to death.
- **Qabalistic qlipha:** Samael – the "shell" of Mercurian forces; name pronounced clearly, hoarsely, and with a hissing S.
- **Operation hours:** 3rd and 10th night hours of Wednesday. (See *Appendix 1 – Hours table* and *Appendix 2 – Hours calculation*)
- **Psychoaromata:** storax (benzoin).
- **Name pronunciation:** name Samigina (or Gamigin), clearly, hoarsely.
- **Pantacular colours:** key-sigil in blue on orange background.
- **Basic colour:** orange.
- **Sound frequencies:** G music note (392 Hz) and C-sharp music note (554 Hz) sounding together.

MARBAS

5

▲ Qliphotic Solarian force in the mental and emotional levels of the neuropsyche, which is to be manifested and controlled; levels identified with the entity-code Marbas.

- **Attainments:** capacity to express sincerity, honesty, and frankness, no matter how painful that may be; development of intelligence to discover and unveil things; ability to maintain good general health (or to recover from illness); ability to optimize physical body and improve its capacity.
- **Qabalistic qlipha:** Thagiriron – the "shell" of Solarian forces; name pronounced clearly, gutturally, and quickly.
- **Operation hours:** 3rd and 10th night hours of Sunday. (See *Appendix 1 – Hours table* and *Appendix 2 – Hours calculation*)
- **Psychoaromata:** spikenard.
- **Name pronunciation:** name Marbas, guttural and fast, with a hissing S.
- **Pantacular colours:** key-sigil in violet on yellow background.
- **Basic colour:** yellow.
- **Sound frequencies:** E music note (330 Hz) and A-sharp music note (466 Hz) sounding together.

VALEFOR

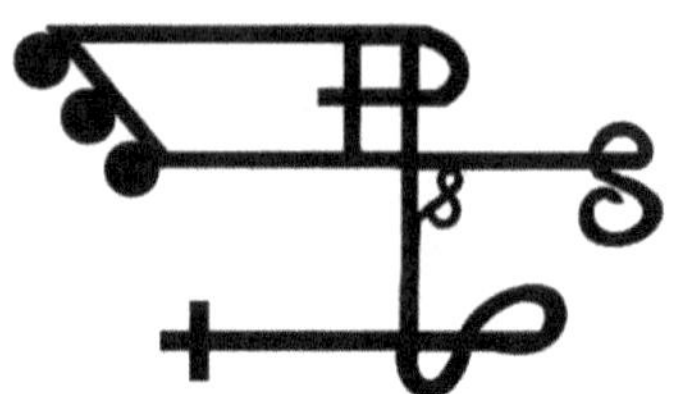

6

▲ Qliphotic Mercurian force in the mental and emotional levels of the neuropsyche, which is to be manifested and controlled; levels identified with the entity-code Valefor.

- **Attainments:** development of cunning and guile sense; ability to sharpen the mind; fast thinking and quick logical reasoning; argumentative ability in order to convince people; skills to deceive, mislead, seduce, delude, steal, elude, and induce people to do the same.
- **Qabalistic qlipha:** Samael – the "shell" of Mercurian forces; name pronounced clearly, hoarsely, and with a hissing S.
- **Operation hours:** 3rd and 10th night hours of Wednesday. (See *Appendix 1 – Hours table* and *Appendix 2 – Hours calculation*)
- **Psychoaromata:** storax (benzoin).
- **Name pronunciation:** name Valefor, guttural, fast clearly, hoarsely.
- **Pantacular colours:** key-sigil in blue on orange background.
- **Basic colour:** orange.
- **Sound frequencies:** G music note (392 Hz) and C-sharp music note (554 Hz) sounding together.

AMON

7

▲ Qliphotic Solarian force in the mental and emotional levels of the neuropsyche, which is to be manifested and controlled; levels identified with the entity-code Amon.

- **Attainments:** social reconciliation and peacemaking skills; ability to guide others to specific objectives; learning from the past; ability to anticipate events.
- **Qabalistic qlipha:** Thagiriron – the "shell" of Solarian forces; name pronounced clearly, gutturally, and quickly.
- **Operation hours:** 3rd and 10th night hours of Sunday. (See *Appendix 1 – Hours table* and *Appendix 2 – Hours calculation*)
- **Psychoaromata:** spikenard.
- **Name pronunciation:** name Amon, guttural and fast.
- **Pantacular colours:** key-sigil in violet on yellow background.
- **Basic colour:** yellow.
- **Sound frequencies:** E music note (330 Hz) and A-sharp music note (466 Hz) sounding together.

BARBATOS

8

▲ Qliphotic Solarian force in the mental and emotional levels of the neuropsyche, which is to be manifested and controlled; levels identified with the entity-code Barbatos.

- **Attainments:** understanding of the verbalized intentions of others; ability to access hidden knowledge; learning from the past; plans for the future; recovery of "lost" friendships; achievement of affection of others for personal purposes.
- **Qabalistic qlipha:** Thagiriron – the "shell" of Solarian forces; name pronounced clearly, gutturally, and quickly.
- **Operation hours:** 3rd and 10th night hours of Sunday. (See *Appendix 1 – Hours table* and *Appendix 2 – Hours calculation*)
- **Psychoaromata:** spikenard.
- **Name pronunciation:** name Barbatos, guttural and fast.
- **Pantacular colours:** key-sigil in violet on yellow background.
- **Basic colour:** yellow.
- **Sound frequencies:** E music note (330 Hz) and A-sharp music note (466 Hz) sounding together.

PAIMON

9

▲ Qliphotic Solarian force in the mental and emotional levels of the neuropsyche, which is to be manifested and controlled; levels identified with the entity-code Paimon.

- **Attainments:** artistic and musical understanding and skills; capacity to learn anything at will; facility for self--motivation; development of a lively and enthusiastic mind; ability to lead and command people; sense of honourableness, fairness, and balance; sense of aesthetics; ability to discover things once hidden or secret.
- **Qabalistic qlipha:** Thagiriron – the "shell" of Solarian forces; name pronounced clearly, gutturally, and quickly.
- **Operation hours:** 3rd and 10th night hours of Sunday. (See *Appendix 1 – Hours table* and *Appendix 2 – Hours calculation*)
- **Psychoaromata:** spikenard.
- **Name pronunciation:** name Paimon, guttural, loud, and fast.
- **Pantacular colours:** key-sigil in violet on yellow background.
- **Basic colour:** yellow.
- **Sound frequencies:** E music note (330 Hz) and A-sharp music note (466 Hz) sounding together.

BUER

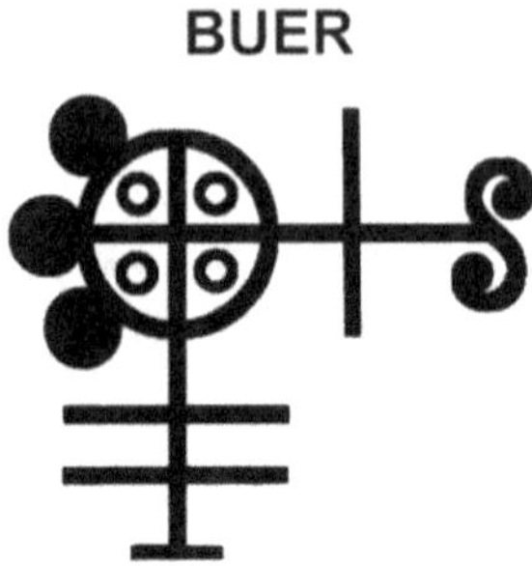

10

▲ Qliphotic Mercurian force in the mental and emotional levels of the neuropsyche, which is to be manifested and controlled; levels identified with the entity-code Buer.

- **Attainments:** emotional-intellective self-control; mastery over emotional impulsive reactivity in acts of provocation and situation of tension; logical reasoning and argumentative skills; philosophical reflection for practical purposes; ability to assimilate knowledge about plants nature and its use for human health.
- **Qabalistic qlipha:** Samael – the "shell" of Mercurian forces; name pronounced clearly, hoarsely, and with a hissing S.
- **Operation hours:** 3rd and 10th night hours of Wednesday. (See *Appendix 1 – Hours table* and *Appendix 2 – Hours calculation*)
- **Psychoaromata:** storax (benzoin).
- **Name pronunciation:** name Buer, clearly, hoarsely.
- **Pantacular colours:** key-sigil in blue on orange background.
- **Basic colour:** orange.
- **Sound frequencies:** G music note (392 Hz) and C-sharp music note (554 Hz) sounding together.

GUSION

11

▲ Qliphotic Solarian force in the mental and emotional levels of the neuropsyche, which is to be manifested and controlled; levels identified with the entity-code Gusion.

- **Attainments:** strengthening of will; ability to get answers and solve problems; learning from the past; ability to make plans; sense of honourableness and respect; skill to regain friendships; ability to get social recognition.
- **Qabalistic qlipha:** Thagiriron – the "shell" of Solarian forces; name pronounced clearly, gutturally, and quickly.
- **Operation hours:** 3rd and 10th night hours of Sunday. (See *Appendix 1 – Hours table* and *Appendix 2 – Hours calculation*)
- **Psychoaromata:** spikenard.
- **Name pronunciation:** name Gusion, guttural and fast, with a hissing S.
- **Pantacular colours:** key-sigil in violet on yellow background.
- **Basic colour:** yellow.
- **Sound frequencies:** E music note (330 Hz) and A-sharp music note (466 Hz) sounding together.

SITRI

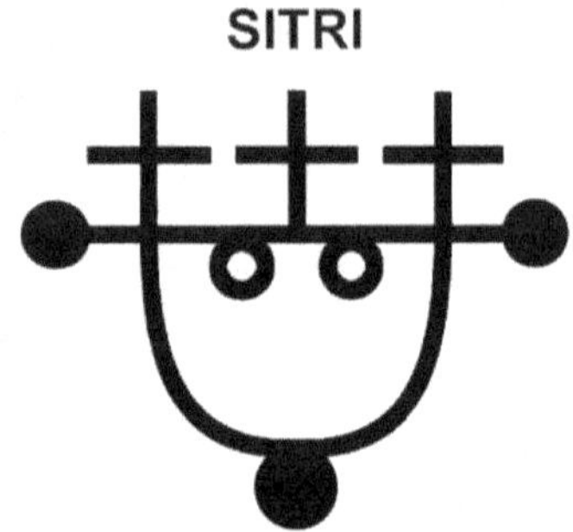

12

▲ Qliphotic Venusian force in the mental and emotional levels of the neuropsyche, which is to be manifested and controlled; levels identified with the entity-code Sitri.

- **Attainments:** ability to arouse passion and love in people; seductive skills; control of imagination and erotic fantasy, in oneself and in others; power to cause fascination through appearances and generate romantic illusion; self-defense against the illusions of passion and "beauty"; development of aesthetic perception.
- **Qabalistic qlipha:** A'arab Zaraq – the "shell" of Venusian forces; name pronounced raspy, gutturally, with a buzzing Z.
- **Operation hours:** 3rd and 10th night hours of Friday. (See *Appendix 1 – Hours table* and *Appendix 2 – Hours calculation*)
- **Psychoaromata:** rose.
- **Name pronunciation:** name Sitri, clearly, raspy, almost a whisper, with a hissing S.
- **Pantacular colours:** key-sigil in red on green background.
- **Basic colour:** green.
- **Sound frequencies:** F music note (349 Hz) and B music note (494 Hz) sounding together.

BELETH

13

▲ Qliphotic Solarian force in the mental and emotional levels of the neuropsyche, which is to be manifested and controlled; levels identified with the entity-code Beleth.

- **Attainments:** development of a sense of politeness and kindness; capacity to identify vanity, jealousy, and arrogance; ability to learn musical arts for the purposes of romantic and social seduction; learning about social and amorous conquest; ability to arouse love and romanticism in people.
- **Qabalistic qlipha:** Thagiriron – the "shell" of Solarian forces; name pronounced clearly, gutturally, and quickly.
- **Operation hours:** 3rd and 10th night hours of Sunday. (See *Appendix 1 – Hours table* and *Appendix 2 – Hours calculation*)
- **Psychoaromata:** spikenard.
- **Name pronunciation:** name Beleth, slightly hoarse, yet pleasant.
- **Pantacular colours:** key-sigil in violet on yellow background.
- **Basic colour:** yellow.
- **Sound frequencies:** E music note (330 Hz) and A-sharp music note (466 Hz) sounding together.

LERAIE

14

▲ Qliphotic Neptunian force in the mental and emotional levels of the neuropsyche, which is to be manifested and controlled; levels identified with the entity-code Leraie.

- **Attainments:** ability to generate emotions that cause struggle and hurt feelings and to cause conflicts that can become serious; ability to cause emotional distress in people; bursts of aggressive insolence.
- **Qabalistic qlipha:** Ghogiel – the "shell" of Neptunian forces; name pronounced deeply, strongly, gutturally, and quickly.
- **Operation hours:** 3rd and 10th night hours of Thursday. (See *Appendix 1 – Hours table* and *Appendix 2 – Hours calculation*)
- **Psychoaromata:** ginger.
- **Name pronunciation:** name Leraie, guttural and fast.
- **Pantacular colours:** key-sigil in dark brown on grey background.
- **Basic colour:** grey.
- **Sound frequencies:** C music note (523 Hz) and F-sharp music note (740 Hz) sounding together.

ELIGOS

15

▲ Qliphotic Jupiterian force in the mental and emotional levels of the neuropsyche, which is to be manifested and controlled; levels identified with the entity-code Eligos.

- **Attainments:** ability to manage finances and business (including military and strategist-minded management); diplomatic skills in the face of conflictive and tense situations; ability to anticipate events; capacity to delegate actions; ability to persuade and get important favours; capacity to identify hypocritical complacency in others.
- **Qabalistic qlipha:** Gha'aseklah – the "shell" of Jupiterian forces; name pronounced clearly, deeply, strongly, with a sizzling S.
- **Operation hours:** 3rd and 10th night hours of Thursday. (See *Appendix 1 – Hours table* and *Appendix 2 – Hours calculation*)
- **Psychoaromata:** nutmeg.
- **Name pronunciation:** name Eligos, clear and strong.
- **Pantacular colours:** key-sigil in orange on blue background.
- **Basic colour:** blue.
- **Sound frequencies:** C music note (262 Hz) and F-sharp music note (370 Hz) sounding together.

ZEPAR

16

▲ Qliphotic Venusian force in the mental and emotional levels of the neuropsyche, which is to be manifested and controlled; levels identified with the entity-code Zepar.

- **Attainments:** seductive skills and ability to arouse passion and love in women; capacity to increase sexual attraction, with no desire or no intent to procreate intentions (in oneself and in women).
- **Qabalistic qlipha:** A'arab Zaraq – the "shell" of Venusian forces; name pronounced raspy, gutturally, with a buzzing Z.
- **Operation hours:** 3rd and 10th night hours of Friday. (See *Appendix 1 – Hours table* and *Appendix 2 – Hours calculation*)
- **Psychoaromata:** rose.
- **Name pronunciation:** name Zepar, clearly, raspy, almost a whisper, with a buzzing Z.
- **Pantacular colours:** key-sigil in red on green background.
- **Basic colour:** green.
- **Sound frequencies:** F music note (349 Hz) and B music note (494 Hz) sounding together.

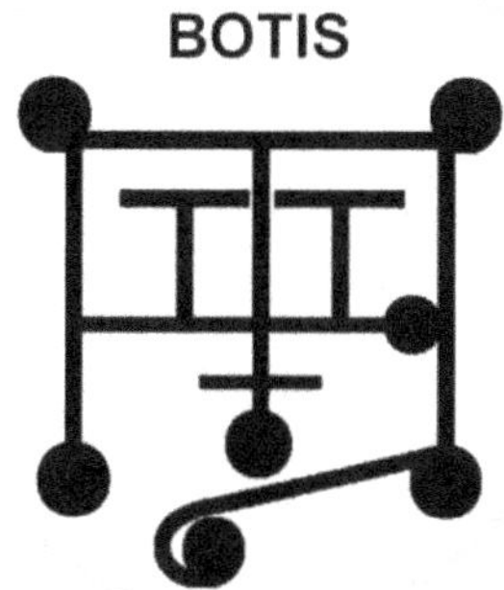

17

▲ Qliphotic Mercurian force in the mental and emotional levels of the neuropsyche, which is to be manifested and controlled; levels identified with the entity-code Botis.

- **Attainments:** maledictive and slanderous power to cause discord; tranquility and mental and emotional self-defense in the face of malevolence; learning from the past; plans for the future; peacemaking skills; ability to regain friend-ships.
- **Qabalistic qlipha:** Samael – the "shell" of Mercurian forces; name pronounced clearly, hoarsely, and with a hissing S.
- **Operation hours:** 3rd and 10th night hours of Wednes-day. (See *Appendix 1 – Hours table* and *Appendix 2 – Hours calculation*)
- **Psychoaromata:** storax (benzoin).
- **Name pronunciation:** name Botis, clearly, hoarsely, suddenly, with an explosive B and a hissing S.
- **Pantacular colours:** key-sigil in blue on orange back-ground.
- **Basic colour:** orange.
- **Sound frequencies:** G music note (392 Hz) and C-sharp music note (554 Hz) sounding together.

BATHIN

18

▲ Qliphotic Terrestrian force in the mental and emotional levels of the neuropsyche, which is to be manifested and controlled; levels identified with the entity-code Bathin.

- **Attainments:** ease of commuting, travel, and transportation; ability to use wisely the available wealth and natural resources; ability to learn and develop the knowledge of mineral and plant nature; interest and easy learning of geography.
- **Qabalistic qlipha:** Lilith – the "shell" of Terrestrian forces; name pronounced deeply, slightly guttural, and slowly.
- **Operation hours:** 3rd and 10th night hours of Saturday. (See *Appendix 1 – Hours table* and *Appendix 2 – Hours calculation*)
- **Psychoaromata:** myrrh.
- **Name pronunciation:** name Bathin, slightly guttural, with an explosive B.
- **Pantacular colours:** key-sigil in purple, crimson, olive green, and white striped on ochre yellow, rust red, and black background.
- **Basic colour:** black.
- **Sound frequencies:** B music note (494 Hz) and F music note (699 Hz) sounding together.

SALLOS

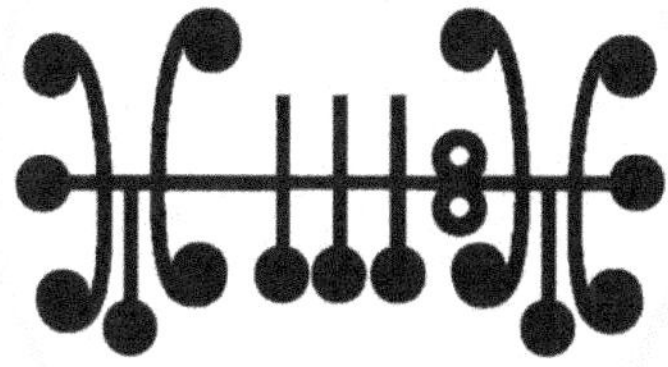

19

▲ Qliphotic Venusian force in the mental and emotional levels of the neuropsyche, which is to be manifested and controlled; levels identified with the entity-code Sallos.

- **Attainments:** seductive skills; ability to arouse sexual passion and love in others; ability to find someone who values fidelity; peacemaking skills in the romantic love context.
- **Qabalistic qlipha:** A'arab Zaraq – the "shell" of Venusian forces; name pronounced raspy, gutturally, with a buzzing Z.
- **Operation hours:** 3rd and 10th night hours of Friday. (See *Appendix 1 – Hours table* and *Appendix 2 – Hours calculation*)
- **Psychoaromata:** rose.
- **Name pronunciation:** name Sallos, or Saleos, clearly, raspy, almost a whisper, with a hissing S.
- **Pantacular colours:** key-sigil in red on green background.
- **Basic colour:** green.
- **Sound frequencies:** F music note (349 Hz) and B music note (494 Hz) sounding together.

PURSON

20

▲ Qliphotic Solarian force in the mental and emotional levels of the neuropsyche, which is to be manifested and controlled; levels identified with the entity-code Purson.

- **Attainments:** ability to get answers about life and the world and come to one's own conclusion; development of discernment; ability to get informations once "secret" or confidential; discoveries of the past; ability to anticipate events.
- **Qabalistic qlipha:** Thagiriron – the "shell" of Solarian forces; name pronounced clearly, gutturally, and quickly.
- **Operation hours:** 3rd and 10th night hours of Sunday. (See *Appendix 1 – Hours table* and *Appendix 2 – Hours calculation*)
- **Psychoaromata:** spikenard.
- **Name pronunciation:** name Purson, guttural and fast.
- **Pantacular colours:** key-sigil in violet on yellow background.
- **Basic colour:** yellow.
- **Sound frequencies:** E music note (330 Hz) and A-sharp music note (466 Hz) sounding together.

MARAX

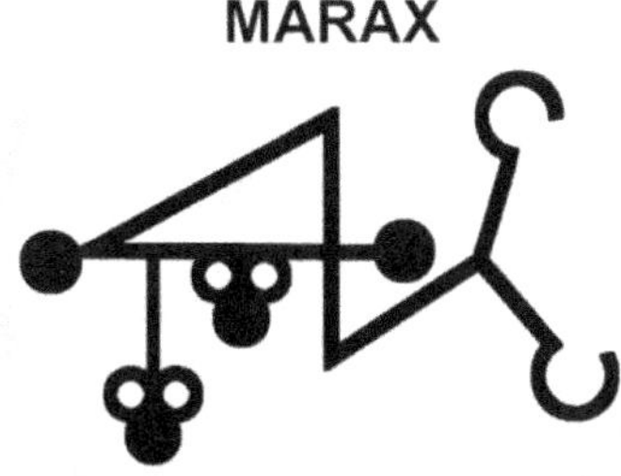

21

▲ Qliphotic Uranian force in the mental and emotional levels of the neuropsyche, which is to be manifested and controlled; levels identified with the entity-code Marax.

- **Attainments:** ability to learn any sciences and arts, especially geometry, arithmetic, astronomy, music, grammar, logic, rhetoric, and plant and mineral sciences; capacity to use wisely the available wealth and natural resources.
- **Qabalistic qlipha:** Da'ath (also a sephira of the same name) – the "shell" of Uranian forces; name pronounced gutturally, and slowly.
- **Operation hours:** 1st night hour, at twilight, any day of the week. (See *Appendix 1 – Hours table* and *Appendix 2 – Hours calculation*)
- **Psychoaromata:** benzoin (1 part) and frankincense (1 part).
- **Name pronunciation:** name Marax, deeply, loudly, with the X sounding /ks/.
- **Pantacular colours:** key-sigil in yellowish grey on purplish grey background.
- **Basic colour:** purplish grey.
- **Sound frequencies:** B-flat/A-sharp music note (466 Hz) and E music note (660 Hz) sounding together.

IPOS

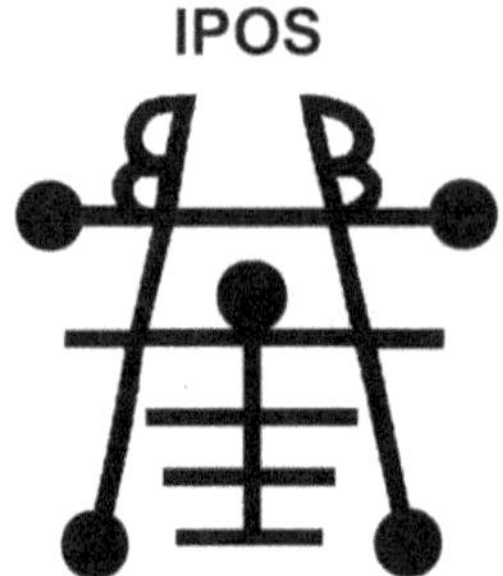

22

▲ Qliphotic Solarian force in the mental and emotional levels of the neuropsyche, which is to be manifested and controlled; levels identified with the entity-code Ipos.

- **Attainments:** ability to get quick understanding (in the present moment) of the events; sensitive perception of situations; strengthening of courage; bursts of bravery; memory of the past (for learning); plans for the future; anticipation of events; sense of renewal after tribulations.
- **Qabalistic qlipha:** Thagiriron – the "shell" of Solarian forces; name pronounced clearly, gutturally, and quickly.
- **Operation hours:** 3rd and 10th night hours of Sunday. (See *Appendix 1 – Hours table* and *Appendix 2 – Hours calculation*)
- **Psychoaromata:** spikenard.
- **Name pronunciation:** name Ipos, guttural and fast.
- **Pantacular colours:** key-sigil in violet on yellow background.
- **Basic colour:** yellow.
- **Sound frequencies:** E music note (330 Hz) and A-sharp music note (466 Hz) sounding together.

AIM

23

▲ Qliphotic Martian force in the mental and emotional levels of the neuropsyche, which is to be manifested and controlled; levels identified with the entity-code Aim.

- **Attainments:** energetic and forceful solution of personal problems; development of malice and cunning sense and cleverness; ability to plan destructive events; capacity to use aggressive force when necessary; ability to get confidential informations.
- **Qabalistic qlipha:** Golachab – the "shell" of Martian forces; name pronounced gutturally, quickly, with CH sounding like an aspirated /h/.
- **Operation hours:** 3rd and 10th night hours of Tuesday. (See *Appendix 1 – Hours table* and *Appendix 2 – Hours calculation*)
- **Psychoaromata:** cofee.
- **Name pronunciation:** name Aim, suddenly, quickly, gutturally.
- **Pantacular colours:** key-sigil in green on red background.
- **Basic colour:** red.
- **Sound frequencies:** D music note (294 Hz) and G-sharp music note (415 Hz) sounding together.

NABERIUS

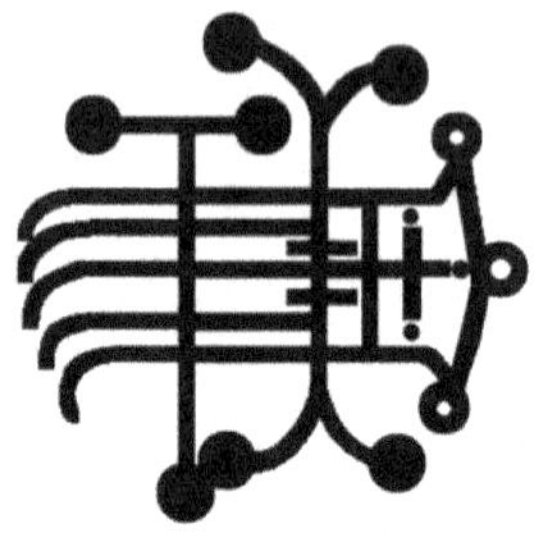

24

▲ Qliphotic Mercurian force in the mental and emotional levels of the neuropsyche, which is to be manifested and controlled; levels identified with the entity-code Naberius.

- **Attainments:** ability to learn easily any science or art; development of eloquence; argumentation skills; sense of dignity; recovery of self-respect and dignity in face of the family and society.
- **Qabalistic qlipha:** Samael – the "shell" of Mercurian forces; name pronounced clearly, hoarsely, and with a hissing S.
- **Operation hours:** 3rd and 10th night hours of Wednesday. (See *Appendix 1 – Hours table* and *Appendix 2 – Hours calculation*)
- **Psychoaromata:** storax (benzoin).
- **Name pronunciation:** name Naberius, clearly, raspy, almost a whisper.
- **Pantacular colours:** key-sigil in blue on orange background.
- **Basic colour:** orange.
- **Sound frequencies:** G music note (392 Hz) and C-sharp music note (554 Hz) sounding together.

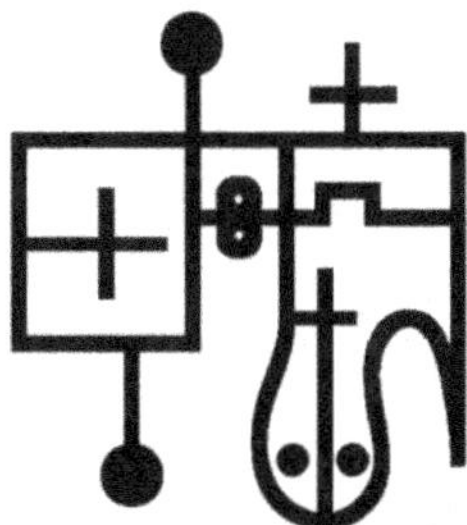

25

▲ Qliphotic Plutonian force in the mental and emotional levels of the neuropsyche, which is to be manifested and controlled; levels identified with the entity-code Glasya-Labolas.

- **Attainments:** capacity to understand easily and immediately any information; ease of learning any sciences; ability for sneaky and furtive behavior to act quietly, cautiously, and discreetly; capacity to incite violence and aggressive impulses in others; ability to arouse love where there is enmity.
- **Qabalistic qlipha:** Thaumiel – the "shell" of Plutonian forces; name pronounced clearly, strongly, gutturally, and quickly.
- **Operation hours:** 3rd and 10th night hours, any day of the week. (See *Appendix 1 – Hours table* and *Appendix 2 – Hours calculation*)
- **Psychoaromata:** camphor.
- **Name pronunciation:** name Glasya-Labolas, suddenly, clearly, gutturally.
- **Pantacular colours:** key-sigil in black on white background.
- **Basic colour:** white.
- **Sound frequencies:** D music note (587 Hz) and G-sharp music note (831 Hz) sounding together.

BUNE

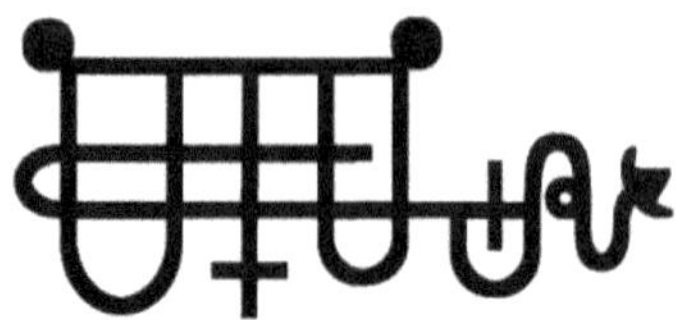

26

▲ Qliphotic Plutonian force in the mental and emotional levels of the neuropsyche, which is to be manifested and controlled; levels identified with the entity-code Bune.

- **Attainments:** capacity to know that there are opportunities to get knowledge, at any time, in any context; development of information immediate understanding; ability to argue about something and convince others; ability to get answers to solve problems; control over the dark and undesirable aspects of mind without misgivings and fears; ability to detach from the deceased people and to be reassured despite the memories.
- **Qabalistic qlipha:** Thaumiel – the "shell" of Plutonian forces; name pronounced clearly, strongly, gutturally, and quickly.
- **Operation hours:** 3rd and 10th night hours, any day of the week. (See *Appendix 1 – Hours table* and *Appendix 2 – Hours calculation*)
- **Psychoaromata:** camphor.
- **Name pronunciation:** name Bune, or Bime, suddenly, clearly, loudly.
- **Pantacular colours:** key-sigil in black on white background.
- **Basic colour:** white.
- **Sound frequencies:** D music note (587 Hz) and G-sharp music note (831 Hz) sounding together.

RONOVE

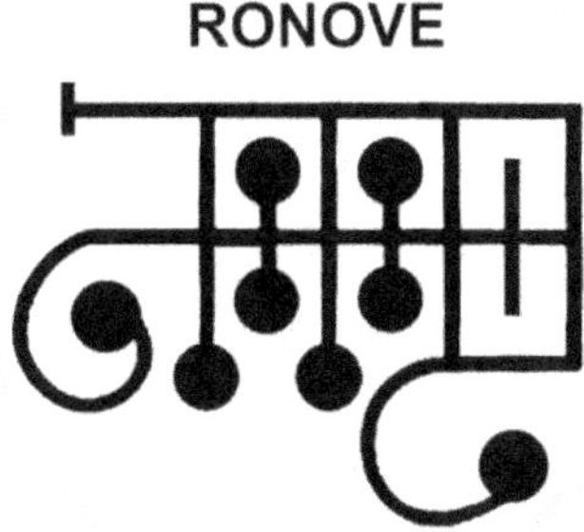

27

▲ Qliphotic Mercurian force in the mental and emotional levels of the neuropsyche, which is to be manifested and controlled; levels identified with the entity-code Ronove.

- **Attainments:** language learning; development of eloquence and argumentation skills; ability to persuade and get favours or advantages from friends or enemies.
- **Qabalistic qlipha:** Samael – the "shell" of Mercurian forces; name pronounced clearly, hoarsely, and with a hissing S.
- **Operation hours:** 3rd and 10th night hours of Wednesday. (See *Appendix 1 – Hours table* and *Appendix 2 – Hours calculation*)
- **Psychoaromata:** storax (benzoin).
- **Name pronunciation:** name Ronove, clearly, raspy.
- **Pantacular colours:** key-sigil in blue on orange background.
- **Basic colour:** orange.
- **Sound frequencies:** G music note (392 Hz) and C-sharp music note (554 Hz) sounding together.

BERITH

28

▲ Qliphotic Solarian force in the mental and emotional levels of the neuropsyche, which is to be manifested and controlled; levels identified with the entity-code Berith.

- **Attainments:** development of creativity; ability to learn from failures and expand self-awareness (in the midst of unfavourable conditions); past knowledge (for learning); plans for the future; ability to earn respect (honestly or otherwise); capacity to commit fallacies intentionaly and lie (masterfully); ability to see through the lies of others.
- **Qabalistic qlipha:** Thagiriron – the "shell" of Solarian forces; name pronounced clearly, gutturally, and quickly.
- **Operation hours:** 3rd and 10th night hours of Sunday. (See *Appendix 1 – Hours table* and *Appendix 2 – Hours calculation*)
- **Psychoaromata:** spikenard.
- **Name pronunciation:** name Berith, or Bolfry, clearly, raspy.
- **Pantacular colours:** key-sigil in violet on yellow background.
- **Basic colour:** yellow.
- **Sound frequencies:** E music note (330 Hz) and A-sharp music note (466 Hz) sounding together.

ASTAROTH

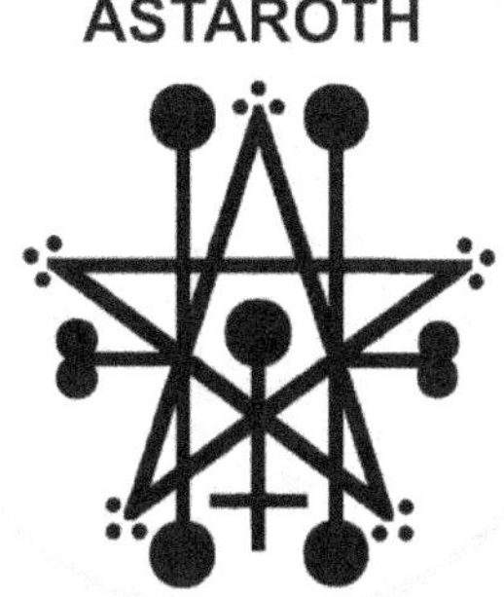

29

▲ Qliphotic Venusian force in the mental and emotional levels of the neuropsyche, which is to be manifested and controlled; levels identified with the entity-code Astaroth.

- **Attainments:** seductive skills (not necessarily sexual skills); development of sarcasm and criticism; rebellious surge (intentionally); understanding of the action-reaction and its conscious use (for good or for bad); learning from the past; plans for the future; ability to get confidential informations or "secrets"; ability to learn and develop rhetoric, logic, and music.
- **Qabalistic qlipha:** A'arab Zaraq – the "shell" of Venusian forces; name pronounced raspy, gutturally, with a buzzing Z.
- **Operation hours:** 3rd and 10th night hours of Friday. (See *Appendix 1 – Hours table* and *Appendix 2 – Hours calculation*)
- **Psychoaromata:** rose.
- **Name pronunciation:** name Astaroth, clearly, raspy, almost a whisper, with a hissing S.
- **Pantacular colours:** key-sigil in red on green background.
- **Basic colour:** green.
- **Sound frequencies:** F music note (349 Hz) and B music note (494 Hz) sounding together.

FORNEUS

30

▲ Qliphotic Neptunian force in the mental and emotional levels of the neuropsyche, which is to be manifested and controlled; levels identified with the entity-code Forneus.

- **Attainments:** real-time argumentative thinking flow; wisdom to deal with different languages at the time of communication; capacity to regain friendships; ability to cause the admiration of friends and enemies.
- **Qabalistic qlipha:** Ghogiel – the "shell" of Neptunian forces; name pronounced deeply, strongly, gutturally, and quickly.
- **Operation hours:** 3rd and 10th night hours of Thursday. (See *Appendix 1 – Hours table* and *Appendix 2 – Hours calculation*)
- **Psychoaromata:** ginger.
- **Name pronunciation:** name Forneus, guttural and fast.
- **Pantacular colours:** key-sigil in dark brown on grey background.
- **Basic colour:** grey.
- **Sound frequencies:** C music note (523 Hz) and F-sharp music note (740 Hz) sounding together.

FORAS

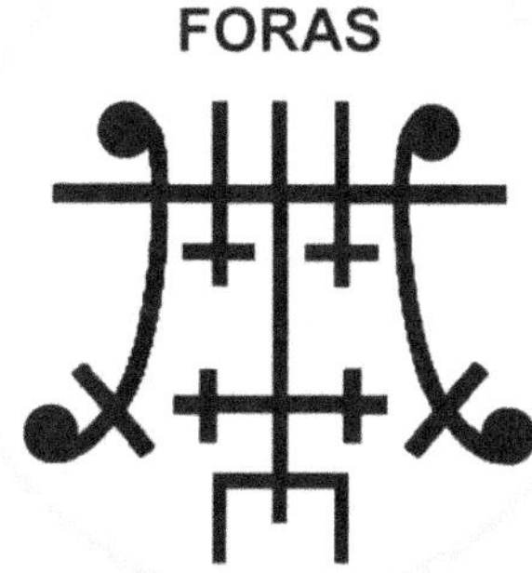

31

▲ Qliphotic Plutonian force in the mental and emotional levels of the neuropsyche, which is to be manifested and controlled; levels identified with the entity-code Foras.

- **Attainments:** capacity to take austere and serious attitude when necessary; ability for sneaky and furtive behavior to act discreetly; knowledge of informations once hidden; sudden useful ideas; capacity to rescue mental and emotional values once lost; ability to recover goods; indomitable behavior; persistence; ability to learn rhetoric, logic, ethics, and natural sciences (plant and mineral); ability to use wisely the available wealth and natural resources.
- **Qabalistic qlipha:** Thaumiel – the "shell" of Plutonian forces; name pronounced clearly, strongly, gutturally, and quickly.
- **Operation hours:** 3rd and 10th night hours, any day of the week.
- **Psychoaromata:** camphor.
- **Name pronunciation:** name Foras, suddenly, gutturaly, clearly.
- **Pantacular colours:** key-sigil in black on white background.
- **Basic colour:** white.
- **Sound frequencies:** D music note (587 Hz) and G-sharp music note (831 Hz) sounding together.

ASMODAI

32

▲ Qliphotic Martian force in the mental and emotional levels of the neuropsyche, which is to be manifested and controlled; levels identified with the entity-code Asmodai.

- **Attainments:** capacity to control anger and direct it when necessary; ability to incite anger and rage in others; persistence and indomitable force; will to act and do things for oneself; energetic and forceful attitude; development of manual skills; ability to learn exact sciences; ability to recover what was lost.
- **Qabalistic qlipha:** Golachab – the "shell" of Martian forces; name pronounced gutturally, quickly, with CH sounding like an aspirated /h/.
- **Operation hours:** 3rd and 10th night hours of Tuesday. (See *Appendix 1 – Hours table* and *Appendix 2 – Hours calculation*)
- **Psychoaromata:** cofee.
- **Name pronunciation:** name Asmodai, suddenly, gutturally.
- **Pantacular colours:** key-sigil in green on red background.
- **Basic colour:** red.
- **Sound frequencies:** D music note (294 Hz) and G-sharp music note (415 Hz) sounding together.

GAAP

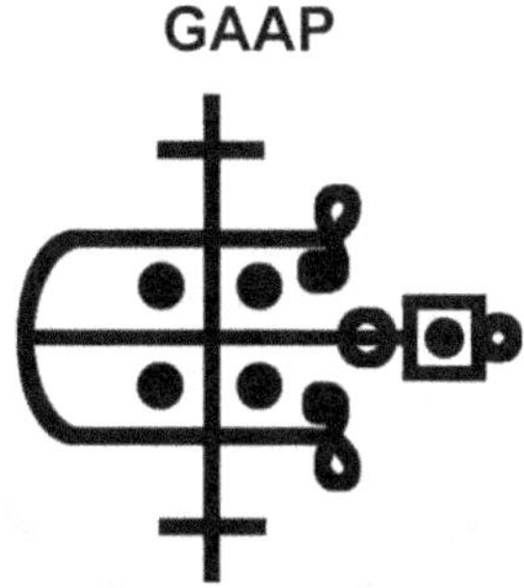

33

▲ Qliphotic Mercurian force in the mental and emotional levels of the neuropsyche, which is to be manifested and controlled; levels identified with the entity-code Gaap.

- **Attainments:** ability to learn exact sciences, human sciences, and arts; capacity to understand different philosophical trends; capacity to elevate reason above emotion; ability to lead debates and conversations and get knowledge out of interlocutors; learning from the past and planning for the future; capacity to arouse love and hatred in others; ability to lead people to acquire knowledge and manipulate them to remain ignorant.
- **Qabalistic qlipha:** Samael – the "shell" of Mercurian forces; name pronounced clearly, hoarsely, and with a hissing S.
- **Operation hours:** 3rd and 10th night hours of Wednesday.
- **Psychoaromata:** storax (benzoin).
- **Name pronunciation:** name Gaap, or Goap, clearly, raspy.
- **Pantacular colours:** key-sigil in blue on orange background.
- **Basic colour:** orange.
- **Sound frequencies:** G music note (392 Hz) and C-sharp music note (554 Hz) sounding together.

FURFUR

34

▲ Qliphotic Jupiterian force in the mental and emotional levels of the neuropsyche, which is to be manifested and controlled; levels identified with the entity-code Furfur.

- **Attainments:** capacity to obtain answers and solutions after difficulties; capacity to discover things for oneself; strong mental stimulation and generation of intense thoughts and chaotic ideas (to organize and apply at will); capacity to arouse philanthropic love and romantic love; social and diplomatic skills.
- **Qabalistic qlipha:** Gha'aseklah – the "shell" of Jupiterian forces; name pronounced clearly, deeply, strongly, with a sizzling S.
- **Operation hours:** 3rd and 10th night hours of Thursday. (See *Appendix 1 – Hours table* and *Appendix 2 – Hours calculation*)
- **Psychoaromata:** nutmeg.
- **Name pronunciation:** name Furfur, raspy, clearly, strongly.
- **Pantacular colours:** key-sigil in orange on blue background.
- **Basic colour:** blue.
- **Sound frequencies:** C music note (262 Hz) and F-sharp music note (370 Hz) sounding together.

MARCHOSIAS

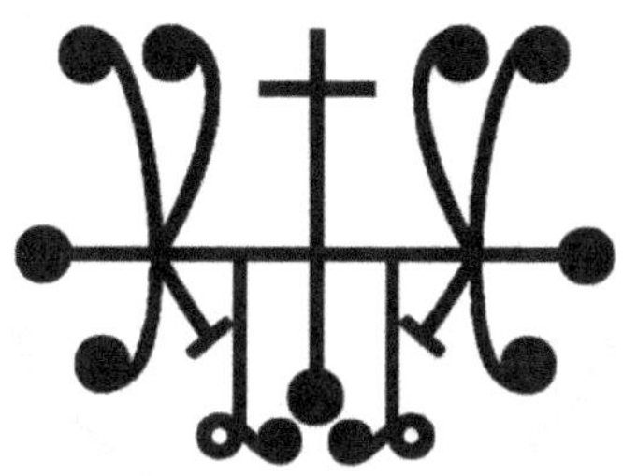

35

▲ Qliphotic Martian force in the mental and emotional levels of the neuropsyche, which is to be manifested and controlled; levels identified with the entity-code Marchosias.

- **Attainments:** strengthening of willpower to fight (physically, verbally, ideologically, professionally, etc.); confrontation capacity; aggressive impulse; energetic and forceful actions; capacity for efforts and resistance to efforts.
- **Qabalistic qlipha:** Golachab – the "shell" of Martian forces; name pronounced gutturally, quickly, with CH sounding like an aspirated /h/.
- **Operation hours:** 3rd and 10th night hours of Tuesday. (See *Appendix 1 – Hours table* and *Appendix 2 – Hours calculation*)
- **Psychoaromata:** cofee.
- **Name pronunciation:** name Marchosias, gutturally, quickly, CH sounding like an aspirated /h/, and with a hissing S.
- **Pantacular colours:** key-sigil in green on red background.
- **Basic colour:** red.
- **Sound frequencies:** D music note (294 Hz) and G-sharp music note (415 Hz) sounding together.

STOLAS

36

▲ Qliphotic Mercurian force in the mental and emotional levels of the neuropsyche, which is to be manifested and controlled; levels identified with the entity-code Stolas.

- **Attainments:** ability to learn exact sciences, nature sciences.
- **Qabalistic qlipha:** Samael – the "shell" of Mercurian forces; name pronounced clearly, hoarsely, and with a hissing S.
- **Operation hours:** 3rd and 10th night hours of Wednesday.
- **Psychoaromata:** storax (benzoin).
- **Name pronunciation:** name Stolas, clearly, raspy.
- **Pantacular colours:** key-sigil in blue on orange background.
- **Basic colour:** orange.
- **Sound frequencies:** G music note (392 Hz) and C-sharp music note (554 Hz) sounding together.

PHENEX

37

▲ Qliphotic Solarian force in the mental and emotional levels of the neuropsyche, which is to be manifested and controlled; levels identified with the entity-code Phenex.

- **Attainments:** capacity to express one's ideas; development of social skills; ability to listen to other people without eagerness or haste to stand out; willingness to help others; capacity to find answers and solutions to the problems; capacity to learn science and arts (especially poetic literature and vocal music).
- **Qabalistic qlipha:** Thagiriron – the "shell" of Solarian forces; name pronounced clearly, gutturally, and quickly.
- **Operation hours:** 3rd and 10th night hours of Sunday. (See *Appendix 1 – Hours table* and *Appendix 2 – Hours calculation*)
- **Psychoaromata:** spikenard.
- **Name pronunciation:** name Phenex, or Phenix, soft, slightly high-pitched, and fast.
- **Pantacular colours:** key-sigil in violet on yellow background.
- **Basic colour:** yellow.
- **Sound frequencies:** E music note (330 Hz) and A-sharp music note (466 Hz) sounding together.

HALPHAS

38

▲ Qliphotic Martian force in the mental and emotional levels of the neuropsyche, which is to be manifested and controlled; levels identified with the entity-code Halphas.

- **Attainments:** willpower to fight against all obstacles; aggressive impulse; self-defense and attack skills; survival skills.
- **Qabalistic qlipha:** Golachab – the "shell" of Martian forces; name pronounced gutturally, quickly, with CH sounding like an aspirated /h/.
- **Operation hours:** 3rd and 10th night hours of Tuesday. (See *Appendix 1 – Hours table* and *Appendix 2 – Hours calculation*)
- **Psychoaromata:** cofee.
- **Name pronunciation:** name Halphas, or Malthas, gutturally, strongly, H sounding aspirated, and with a hissing S.
- **Pantacular colours:** key-sigil in green on red background.
- **Basic colour:** red.
- **Sound frequencies:** D music note (294 Hz) and G-sharp music note (415 Hz) sounding together.

MALPHAS

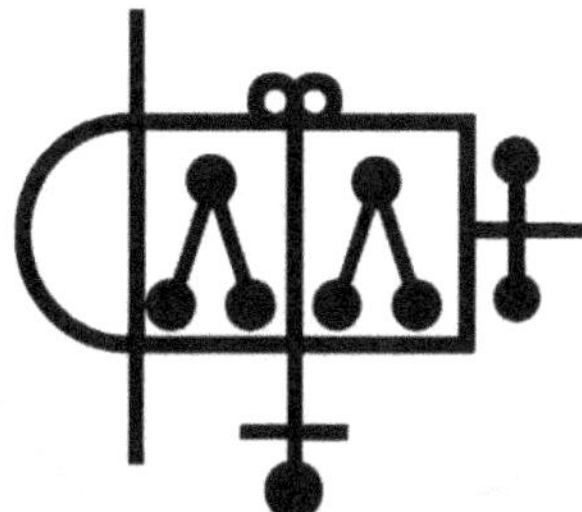

39

▲ Qliphotic Saturnian force in the mental and emotional levels of the neuropsyche, which is to be manifested and controlled; levels identified with the entity-code Malphas.

- **Attainments:** malice and cunning; ability to perceive other people's bad intentions (about what they did or they think about doing); self-defense and protection; capacity to take a lot of effort to get things; ability to hide and keep secrets.
- **Qabalistic qlipha:** Satariel – the "shell" of Saturnian forces; name pronounced strongly, gutturally, slowly, and dolefully.
- **Operation hours:** 3rd and 10th night hours of Saturday. (See *Appendix 1 – Hours table* and *Appendix 2 – Hours calculation*)
- **Psychoaromata:** mandrake; myrrh.
- **Name pronunciation:** name Malphas, gutturally, deeply, strongly, PH sounding like /f/.
- **Pantacular colours:** key-sigil in white on black background.
- **Basic colour:** black.
- **Sound frequencies:** B music note (494 Hz) and F music note (699 Hz) sounding together.

RAUM

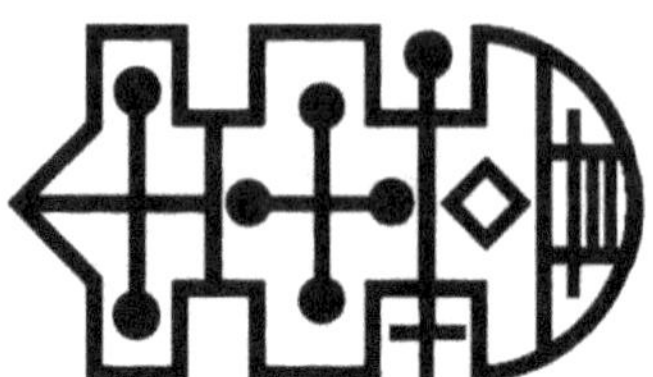

40

▲ Qliphotic Mercurian force in the mental and emotional levels of the neuropsyche, which is to be manifested and controlled; levels identified with the entity-code Raum.

- **Attainments:** ability to invent and propagate fake news about people and places and tarnish the reputation of others; ability to earn trust and admiration of enemies; power to free minds enslaved by supposed authority figures (political or religious); learning from the past; plans for the future; ability to anticipate events.
- **Qabalistic qlipha:** Samael – the "shell" of Mercurian forces; name pronounced clearly, hoarsely, and with a hissing S.
- **Operation hours:** 3rd and 10th night hours of Wednesday.
- **Psychoaromata:** storax (benzoin).
- **Name pronunciation:** name Raum, clearly, raspy.
- **Pantacular colours:** key-sigil in blue on orange background.
- **Basic colour:** orange.
- **Sound frequencies:** G music note (392 Hz) and C-sharp music note (554 Hz) sounding together.

FOCALOR

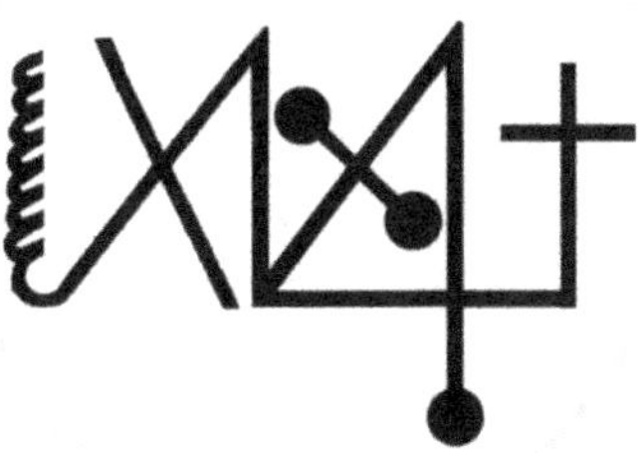

41

▲ Qliphotic Neptunian force in the mental and emotional levels of the neuropsyche, which is to be manifested and controlled; levels identified with the entity-code Focalor.

- **Attainments:** ability to generate intense violent emotional flows in enemy persons (causing them to ruin themselves emotionally and physically); ability to heighten the emotions and thoughts of friends in a beneficial way.
- **Qabalistic qlipha:** Ghogiel – the "shell" of Neptunian forces; name pronounced deeply, strongly, gutturally, and quickly.
- **Operation hours:** 3rd and 10th night hours of Thursday. (See *Appendix 1 – Hours table* and *Appendix 2 – Hours calculation*)
- **Psychoaromata:** ginger.
- **Name pronunciation:** name Focalor, or Furcalor, guttural and fast.
- **Pantacular colours:** key-sigil in dark brown on grey background.
- **Basic colour:** grey.
- **Sound frequencies:** C music note (523 Hz) and F-sharp music note (740 Hz) sounding together.

VEPAR

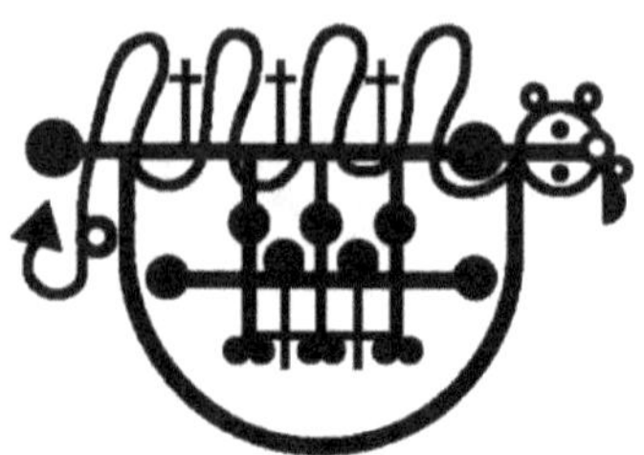

42

▲ Qliphotic Lunarian force in the mental and emotional levels of the neuropsyche, which is to be manifested and controlled; levels identified with the entity-code Vepar.

- **Attainments:** development of strength and emotional resilience to face tribulations; ability to cause chaotic and unstable emotional effects on people; ability to drive the toxic, dangerous and destructive feelings of others according to the will; emotional blackmail skills.
- **Qabalistic qlipha:** Gamaliel – the "shell" of Lunarian forces; name pronounced hoarsely, almost a whisper.
- **Operation hours:** 3rd and 10th night hours of Monday.
- **Psychoaromata:** wormwood.
- **Name pronunciation:** name Vepar, or Separ, raspy, almost a whisper, sustained.
- **Pantacular colours:** key-sigil in yellow on violet background.
- **Basic colour:** violet.
- **Sound frequencies:** A music note (440 Hz) and D-sharp music note (622 Hz) sounding together.

SABNOCK

43

▲ Qliphotic Martian force in the mental and emotional levels of the neuropsyche, which is to be manifested and controlled; levels identified with the entity-code Sabnock.

- **Attainments:** self-defense and violent attack skills; bellicose impetus; survival skills; capacity to learn engineerings.
- **Qabalistic qlipha:** Golachab – the "shell" of Martian forces; name pronounced gutturally, quickly, with CH sounding like an aspirated /h/.
- **Operation hours:** 3rd and 10th night hours of Tuesday. (See *Appendix 1 – Hours table* and *Appendix 2 – Hours calculation*)
- **Psychoaromata:** cofee.
- **Name pronunciation:** name Sabnock, gutturally, strongly, with a hissing S.
- **Pantacular colours:** key-sigil in green on red background.
- **Basic colour:** red.
- **Sound frequencies:** D music note (294 Hz) and G-sharp music note (415 Hz) sounding together.

SHAX

44

▲ Qliphotic Mercurian force in the mental and emotional levels of the neuropsyche, which is to be manifested and controlled; levels identified with the entity-code Shax.

- **Attainments:** ability to stray people from important things and prevent access to knowledge and culture; ability to lie and propagate fake informations on any subject (and keep people in ignorance); power to free minds enslaved by supposed authority figures (political or religious) and to tarnish the honour of supposedly important people; ability to obtain supposedly good people unprotected hidden knowledge; ease of quick transportation and travel when needed.
- **Qabalistic qlipha:** Samael – the "shell" of Mercurian forces; name pronounced clearly, hoarsely, and with a hissing S.
- **Operation hours:** 3rd and 10th night hours of Wednesday.
- **Psychoaromata:** storax (benzoin).
- **Name pronunciation:** name Shax, raspy, with the X sounding /ks/.
- **Pantacular colours:** key-sigil in blue on orange background.
- **Basic colour:** orange.
- **Sound frequencies:** G music note (392 Hz) and C-sharp music note (554 Hz) sounding together.

VINE

45

▲ Qliphotic Martian force in the mental and emotional levels of the neuropsyche, which is to be manifested and controlled; levels identified with the entity-code Vine.

- **Attainments:** self-defense and violent attack skills when needed; ability to provide properties and goods protection; survival skills; ability to stir people's emotions and pit them against each other; capacity to get hidden knowledge and revelations about intentioned persons; learning from the past; planning for the future; engineerings learning.
- **Qabalistic qlipha:** Golachab – the "shell" of Martian forces; name pronounced gutturally, quickly, with CH sounding like an aspirated /h/.
- **Operation hours:** 3rd and 10th night hours of Tuesday. (See *Appendix 1 – Hours table* and *Appendix 2 – Hours calculation*)
- **Psychoaromata:** cofee.
- **Name pronunciation:** name Vine, or Vinea, guttural, strong.
- **Pantacular colours:** key-sigil in green on red background.
- **Basic colour:** red.
- **Sound frequencies:** D music note (294 Hz) and G-sharp music note (415 Hz) sounding together.

BIFRONS

46

▲ Qliphotic Uranian force in the mental and emotional levels of the neuropsyche, which is to be manifested and controlled; levels identified with the entity-code Bifrons.

- **Attainments:** ability to learn any sciences and arts; renewal of memory, recovery of previously forgotten knowledge once forgotten and the ability to make new uses of that knowledge.
- **Qabalistic qlipha:** Da'ath (also a sephira of the same name) – the "shell" of Uranian forces; name pronounced gutturally, and slowly.
- **Operation hours:** 1st night hour, at twilight, any day of the week. (See *Appendix 1 – Hours table* and *Appendix 2 – Hours calculation*)
- **Psychoaromata:** benzoin (1 part) and frankincense (1 part).
- **Name pronunciation:** name Bifrons, deeply, gutturaly, loudly.
- **Pantacular colours:** key-sigil in yellowish grey on purplish grey background.
- **Basic colour:** purplish grey.
- **Sound frequencies:** B-flat/A-sharp music note (466 Hz) and E music note (660 Hz) sounding together.

VUAL

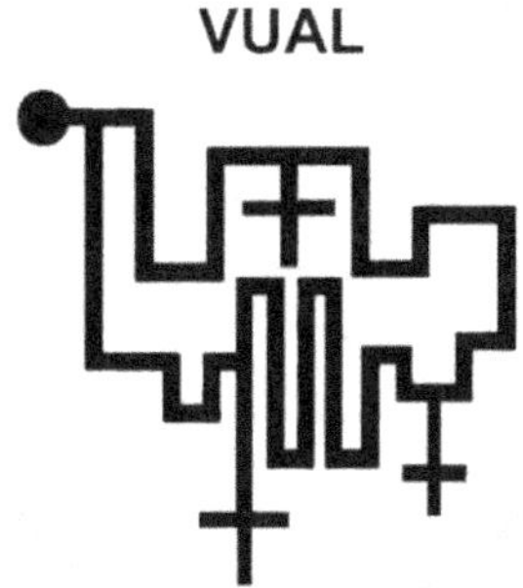

47

▲ Qliphotic Venusian force in the mental and emotional levels of the neuropsyche, which is to be manifested and controlled; levels identified with the entity-code Vual.

- **Attainments:** seductive skills; ability to obtain female love; earning friendship and sympathy of anyone, including supposed enemies; capacity to persuade and obtain favours; ability to create bonds and relationships; learning from the past; planning for the future.
- **Qabalistic qlipha:** A'arab Zaraq – the "shell" of Venusian forces; name pronounced raspy, gutturally, with a buzzing Z.
- **Operation hours:** 3rd and 10th night hours of Friday. (See *Appendix 1 – Hours table* and *Appendix 2 – Hours calculation*)
- **Psychoaromata:** rose.
- **Name pronunciation:** name Vual, or Uval, clearly, raspy, almost a whisper.
- **Pantacular colours:** key-sigil in red on green background.
- **Basic colour:** green.
- **Sound frequencies:** F music note (349 Hz) and B music note (494 Hz) sounding together.

HAAGENTI

48

▲ Qliphotic Solarian force in the mental and emotional levels of the neuropsyche, which is to be manifested and controlled; levels identified with the entity-code Haagenti.

- **Attainments:** ability to change one's mind and thought patterns; capacity to expand self-awareness (in the midst of unfavourable conditions); ability to take advantage of problems to acquire learning and turn them into opportunities; mental and emotional capacities to understand different issues and problems.
- **Qabalistic qlipha:** Thagiriron – the "shell" of Solarian forces; name pronounced clearly, gutturally, and quickly.
- **Operation hours:** 3rd and 10th night hours of Sunday. (See *Appendix 1 – Hours table* and *Appendix 2 – Hours calculation*)
- **Psychoaromata:** spikenard.
- **Name pronunciation:** name Haagenti, guttural and fast.
- **Pantacular colours:** key-sigil in violet on yellow background.
- **Basic colour:** yellow.
- **Sound frequencies:** E music note (330 Hz) and A-sharp music note (466 Hz) sounding together.

CROCEL

49

▲ Qliphotic Jupiterian force in the mental and emotional levels of the neuropsyche, which is to be manifested and controlled; levels identified with the entity-code Crocel.

- **Attainments:** planning skills; capacity to learn geometry, arithmetic, grammar, logic, rhetoric; ability to heighten and inflame people's emotions through elaborate speech; capacity to get hidden information and discover secrets.
- **Qabalistic qlipha:** Gha'aseklah – the "shell" of Jupiterian forces; name pronounced clearly, deeply, strongly, with a sizzling S.
- **Operation hours:** 3rd and 10th night hours of Thursday. (See *Appendix 1 – Hours table* and *Appendix 2 – Hours calculation*)
- **Psychoaromata:** nutmeg.
- **Name pronunciation:** name Crocel, or Procel, deeply, clearly, strongly.
- **Pantacular colours:** key-sigil in orange on blue background.
- **Basic colour:** blue.
- **Sound frequencies:** C music note (262 Hz) and F-sharp music note (370 Hz) sounding together.

FURCAS

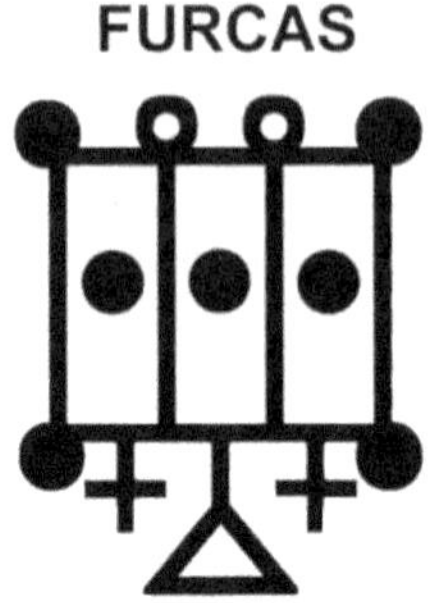

50

▲ Qliphotic Saturnian force in the mental and emotional levels of the neuropsyche, which is to be manifested and controlled; levels identified with the entity-code Furcas.

- **Attainments:** ability to argue about something and convince others; development of logical thinking; intellectual aggressiveness and malice; capacity to learn philosophy in general; development of patience.
- **Qabalistic qlipha:** Satariel – the "shell" of Saturnian forces; name pronounced strongly, gutturally, slowly, and dolefully.
- **Operation hours:** 3rd and 10th night hours of Saturday. (See *Appendix 1 – Hours table* and *Appendix 2 – Hours calculation*)
- **Psychoaromata:** mandrake; myrrh.
- **Name pronunciation:** name Furcas, deep, guttural.
- **Pantacular colours:** key-sigil in white on black background.
- **Basic colour:** black.
- **Sound frequencies:** B music note (494 Hz) and F music note (699 Hz) sounding together.

BALAM

51

▲ Qliphotic Solarian force in the mental and emotional levels of the neuropsyche, which is to be manifested and controlled; levels identified with the entity-code Balam.

- **Attainments:** ability to discover and learn for oneself; willpower to expand intelligence and perception; capacity for prudence; rediscovery of knowledge from the past for application in the present time; ability to plan for the future.
- **Qabalistic qlipha:** Thagiriron – the "shell" of Solarian forces; name pronounced clearly, gutturally, and quickly.
- **Operation hours:** 3rd and 10th night hours of Sunday. (See *Appendix 1 – Hours table* and *Appendix 2 – Hours calculation*)
- **Psychoaromata:** spikenard.
- **Name pronunciation:** name Balam, or Balaam, softly hoarse.
- **Pantacular colours:** key-sigil in violet on yellow background.
- **Basic colour:** yellow.
- **Sound frequencies:** E music note (330 Hz) and A-sharp music note (466 Hz) sounding together.

ALLOCES

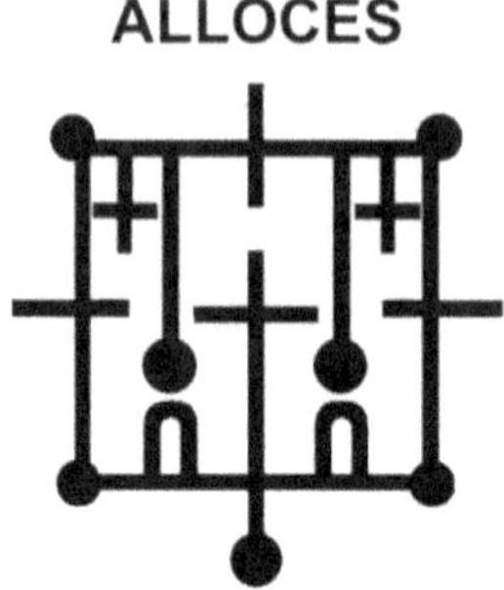

52

▲ Qliphotic Martian force in the mental and emotional levels of the neuropsyche, which is to be manifested and controlled; levels identified with the entity-code Alloces.

- **Attainments:** capacity to learn exact sciences, grammar, logic and rhetoric, with a strategist approach; skills for conflict, combat and fighting; development of a sense of revenge and justice.
- **Qabalistic qlipha:** Golachab – the "shell" of Martian forces; name pronounced gutturally, quickly, with CH sounding like an aspirated /h/.
- **Operation hours:** 3rd and 10th night hours of Tuesday. (See *Appendix 1 – Hours table* and *Appendix 2 – Hours calculation*)
- **Psychoaromata:** cofee.
- **Name pronunciation:** name Alloces, or Alocas, guttural, strong.
- **Pantacular colours:** key-sigil in green on red background.
- **Basic colour:** red.
- **Sound frequencies:** D music note (294 Hz) and G-sharp music note (415 Hz) sounding together.

CAMIO

53

▲ Qliphotic Martian force in the mental and emotional levels of the neuropsyche, which is to be manifested and controlled; levels identified with the entity-code Camio.

- **Attainments:** ability to create and hold impassioned and heated debates; mastery over aggressive impulses; capacity to learn natural and agricultural sciences (uses of natural and technological resources); ability to anticipate events.
- **Qabalistic qlipha:** Golachab – the "shell" of Martian forces; name pronounced gutturally, quickly, with CH sounding like an aspirated /h/.
- **Operation hours:** 3rd and 10th night hours of Tuesday. (See *Appendix 1 – Hours table* and *Appendix 2 – Hours calculation*)
- **Psychoaromata:** cofee.
- **Name pronunciation:** name Camio, or Caim, guttural, strong.
- **Pantacular colours:** key-sigil in green on red background.
- **Basic colour:** red.
- **Sound frequencies:** D music note (294 Hz) and G-sharp music note (415 Hz) sounding together.

MURMUR

54

▲ Qliphotic Saturnian force in the mental and emotional levels of the neuropsyche, which is to be manifested and controlled; levels identified with the entity-code Murmur.

- **Attainments:** capacity to learn philosophy in general and apply it in practical life; ability to recover knowledge once forgotten and bring it to a new understanding and to resolve difficult and painful issues.
- **Qabalistic qlipha:** Satariel – the "shell" of Saturnian forces; name pronounced strongly, gutturally, slowly, and dolefully.
- **Operation hours:** 3rd and 10th night hours of Saturday. (See *Appendix 1 – Hours table* and *Appendix 2 – Hours calculation*)
- **Psychoaromata:** mandrake; myrrh.
- **Name pronunciation:** name Murmur, or Murmus, deep, guttural.
- **Pantacular colours:** key-sigil in white on black background.
- **Basic colour:** black.
- **Sound frequencies:** B music note (494 Hz) and F music note (699 Hz) sounding together.

OROBAS

55

▲ Qliphotic Jupiterian force in the mental and emotional levels of the neuropsyche, which is to be manifested and controlled; levels identified with the entity-code Orobas.

- **Attainments:** ability to persuade and obtain favours from friends or enemies; development of a sense of honour and firmness of character; strength, will and means to obtain social ascension and recognition; ability to protect and preserve goods and assets; learning from the past; planning for the future.
- **Qabalistic qlipha:** Gha'aseklah – the "shell" of Jupiterian forces; name pronounced clearly, deeply, strongly, with a sizzling S.
- **Operation hours:** 3rd and 10th night hours of Thursday. (See *Appendix 1 – Hours table* and *Appendix 2 – Hours calculation*)
- **Psychoaromata:** nutmeg.
- **Name pronunciation:** name Orobas, deeply, clearly, strongly.
- **Pantacular colours:** key-sigil in orange on blue background.
- **Basic colour:** blue.
- **Sound frequencies:** C music note (262 Hz) and F-sharp music note (370 Hz) sounding together.

GREMORY

56

▲ Qliphotic Lunarian force in the mental and emotional levels of the neuropsyche, which is to be manifested and controlled; levels identified with the entity-code Gremory.

- **Attainments:** capacity to get female affection; ability to discover revelations about loving feelings; capacity to value romanticism and persist on love; development of romantic interest in women of various ages, and the ability to arouse love interest in these women; knowledge of things once hidden.
- **Qabalistic qlipha:** Gamaliel – the "shell" of Lunarian forces; name pronounced hoarsely, almost a whisper.
- **Operation hours:** 3rd and 10th night hours of Monday.
- **Psychoaromata:** wormwood.
- **Name pronunciation:** name Gremory, or Gamori, almost a whisper, sustained, with oscillation in volume.
- **Pantacular colours:** key-sigil in yellow on violet background.
- **Basic colour:** violet.
- **Sound frequencies:** A music note (440 Hz) and D-sharp music note (622 Hz) sounding together.

OSE

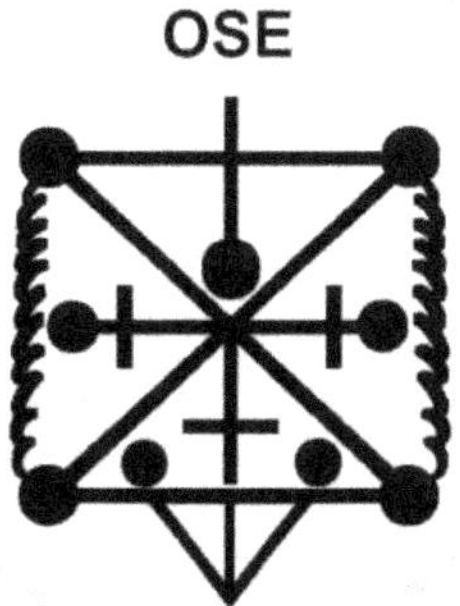

57

▲ Qliphotic Mercurian force in the mental and emotional levels of the neuropsyche, which is to be manifested and controlled; levels identified with the entity-code Ose.

- **Attainments:** ability to pretend to be what one is not; persuasive skills ("brainwashing" people, making them believe they are what they are not); ability to make up elaborate lies and illusions, or undo these lies, to manipulate others; ability to discover secrets or confidential information; capacity to learn exact sciences, philosophy, literature, grammar, and languages.
- **Qabalistic qlipha:** Samael – the "shell" of Mercurian forces; name pronounced clearly, hoarsely, and with a hissing S.
- **Operation hours:** 3rd and 10th night hours of Wednesday.
- **Psychoaromata:** storax (benzoin).
- **Name pronunciation:** name Ose, or Oso, raspy, with the S sounding /ss/.
- **Pantacular colours:** key-sigil in blue on orange background.
- **Basic colour:** orange.
- **Sound frequencies:** G music note (392 Hz) and C-sharp music note (554 Hz) sounding together.

AMY

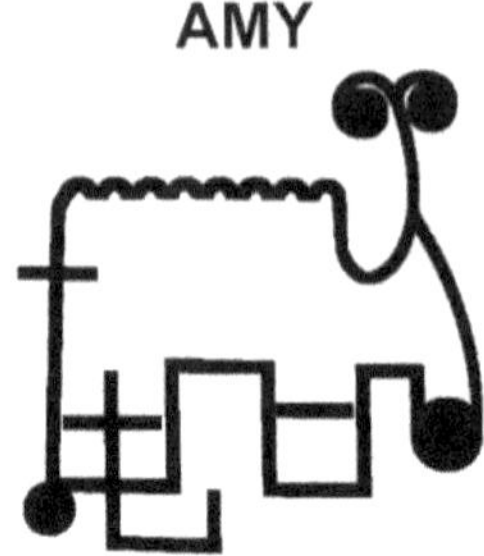

58

▲ Qliphotic Mercurian force in the mental and emotional levels of the neuropsyche, which is to be manifested and controlled; levels identified with the entity-code Amy.

- **Attainments:** capacity to learn exact sciences; persuasive skills; capacity to think rationally; discovery and development of useful new skills.
- **Qabalistic qlipha:** Samael – the "shell" of Mercurian forces; name pronounced clearly, hoarsely, and with a hissing S.
- **Operation hours:** 3rd and 10th night hours of Wednesday.
- **Psychoaromata:** storax (benzoin).
- **Name pronunciation:** name Amy, raspy.
- **Pantacular colours:** key-sigil in blue on orange background.
- **Basic colour:** orange.
- **Sound frequencies:** G music note (392 Hz) and C-sharp music note (554 Hz) sounding together.

ORIAS

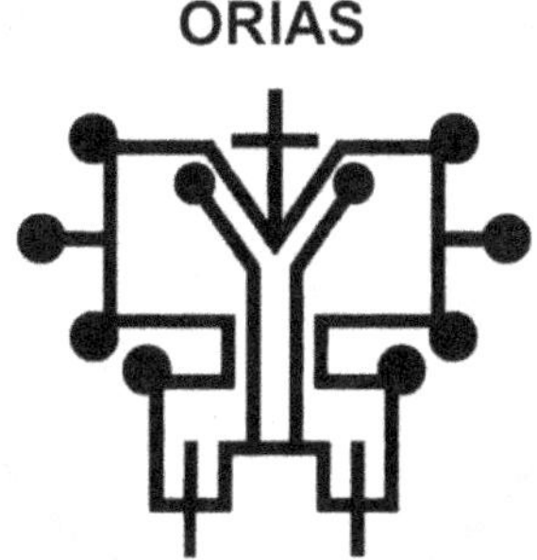

59

▲ Qliphotic Solarian force in the mental and emotional levels of the neuropsyche, which is to be manifested and controlled; levels identified with the entity-code Orias.

- **Attainments:** strength and willpower to achieve social ascension and recognition; development of self-respect and sense of honour; persuasive skills and ability to get favours from friends or enemies; capacity to learn astronomy and exact sciences.
- **Qabalistic qlipha:** Thagiriron – the "shell" of Solarian forces; name pronounced clearly, gutturally, and quickly.
- **Operation hours:** 3rd and 10th night hours of Sunday. (See *Appendix 1 – Hours table* and *Appendix 2 – Hours calculation*)
- **Psychoaromata:** spikenard.
- **Name pronunciation:** name Orias, or Oriax, raspy, with a hissing S, or with X sounding /ks/.
- **Pantacular colours:** key-sigil in violet on yellow background.
- **Basic colour:** yellow.
- **Sound frequencies:** E music note (330 Hz) and A-sharp music note (466 Hz) sounding together.

VAPULA

60

▲ Qliphotic Uranian force in the mental and emotional levels of the neuropsyche, which is to be manifested and controlled; levels identified with the entity-code Vapula.

- **Attainments:** ability to learn and develop any craft, trade, or job, science, art, or philosophy; manual skills.
- **Qabalistic qlipha:** Da'ath (also a sephira of the same name) – the "shell" of Uranian forces; name pronounced gutturally, and slowly.
- **Operation hours:** 1st night hour, at twilight, any day of the week. (See *Appendix 1 – Hours table* and *Appendix 2 – Hours calculation*)
- **Psychoaromata:** benzoin (1 part) and frankincense (1 part).
- **Name pronunciation:** name Vapula, or Nafula, gutturaly, loudly.
- **Pantacular colours:** key-sigil in yellowish grey on purplish grey background.
- **Basic colour:** purplish grey.
- **Sound frequencies:** B-flat/A-sharp music note (466 Hz) and E music note (660 Hz) sounding together.

ZAGAN

61

▲ Qliphotic Solarian force in the mental and emotional levels of the neuropsyche, which is to be manifested and controlled; levels identified with the entity-code Zagan.

- **Attainments:** ability to change patterns of harmful feelings and unhealthy thoughts into productive ones; capacity to expand self-awareness (in the midst of unfavourable conditions); ability to assimilate and adapt knowledge to whatever may be needed; ability to teach and educate others, or to deceive them and keep them in ignorance.
- **Qabalistic qlipha:** Thagiriron – the "shell" of Solarian forces; name pronounced clearly, gutturally, and quickly.
- **Operation hours:** 3rd and 10th night hours of Sunday. (See *Appendix 1 – Hours table* and *Appendix 2 – Hours calculation*)
- **Psychoaromata:** spikenard.
- **Name pronunciation:** name Zagan, raspy and softly.
- **Pantacular colours:** key-sigil in violet on yellow background.
- **Basic colour:** yellow.
- **Sound frequencies:** E music note (330 Hz) and A-sharp music note (466 Hz) sounding together.

VOLAC

62

▲ Qliphotic Uranian force in the mental and emotional levels of the neuropsyche, which is to be manifested and controlled; levels identified with the entity-code Volac.

- **Attainments:** ability to find information amidst the confusion and discern it; ability to identify where there is wisdom and assimilate it without great efforts; self--discovery.
- **Qabalistic qlipha:** Da'ath (also a sephira of the same name) – the "shell" of Uranian forces; name pronounced gutturally, and slowly.
- **Operation hours:** 1st night hour, at twilight, any day of the week. (See *Appendix 1 – Hours table* and *Appendix 2 – Hours calculation*)
- **Psychoaromata:** benzoin (1 part) and frankincense (1 part).
- **Name pronunciation:** name Volac, or Valac, gutturaly, loudly.
- **Pantacular colours:** key-sigil in yellowish grey on purplish grey background.
- **Basic colour:** purplish grey.
- **Sound frequencies:** B-flat/A-sharp music note (466 Hz) and E music note (660 Hz) sounding together.

ANDRAS

63

▲ Qliphotic Martian force in the mental and emotional levels of the neuropsyche, which is to be manifested and controlled; levels identified with the entity-code Andras.

- **Attainments:** ability to cause discord, disagreement, and conflict; ability to arouse fear and paranoia in people; development of a sense of danger (knowing how to identify what is dangerous and using reason to deal with it); possible loss of rational cognition and its consequences.
- **Qabalistic qlipha:** Golachab – the "shell" of Martian forces; name pronounced gutturally, quickly, with CH sounding like an aspirated /h/.
- **Operation hours:** 3rd and 10th night hours of Tuesday. (See *Appendix 1 – Hours table* and *Appendix 2 – Hours calculation*)
- **Psychoaromata:** cofee.
- **Name pronunciation:** name Andras, guttural, strong.
- **Pantacular colours:** key-sigil in green on red background.
- **Basic colour:** red.
- **Sound frequencies:** D music note (294 Hz) and G-sharp music note (415 Hz) sounding together.

HAURES

64

▲ Qliphotic Uranian force in the mental and emotional levels of the neuropsyche, which is to be manifested and controlled; levels identified with the entity-code Haures.

- **Attainments:** discerning ability; intelligence to obtain information amidst the confusion and lies; resistance to illusions of life; cunning and malice; intellectual strength; aggressive argumentation; mental and emotional self-defense; capacity to learn from past mistakes; development of ideas for the future; ability to ruin people's reputations.
- **Qabalistic qlipha:** Da'ath (also a sephira of the same name) – the "shell" of Uranian forces; name pronounced gutturally, and slowly.
- **Operation hours:** 1st night hour, at twilight, any day of the week. (See *Appendix 1 – Hours table* and *Appendix 2 – Hours calculation*)
- **Psychoaromata:** benzoin (1 part) and frankincense (1 part).
- **Name pronunciation:** name Haures, or Hauras, gutturaly, loudly, with H sounding aspirated.
- **Pantacular colours:** key-sigil in yellowish grey on purplish grey background.
- **Basic colour:** purplish grey.
- **Sound frequencies:** B-flat/A-sharp music note (466 Hz) and E music note (660 Hz) sounding together.

ANDREALPHUS

65

▲ Qliphotic Mercurian force in the mental and emotional levels of the neuropsyche, which is to be manifested and controlled; levels identified with the entity-code Andrealphus.

- **Attainments:** capacity to learn and teach exact sciences; capacity to expand intellectual creativity; sense of intellectual freedom; creative use of imagination, without dogmas or taboos; defense against intellectual, rhetorical, and fallacious attacks.
- **Qabalistic qlipha:** Samael – the "shell" of Mercurian forces; name pronounced clearly, hoarsely, and with a hissing S.
- **Operation hours:** 3rd and 10th night hours of Wednesday.
- **Psychoaromata:** storax (benzoin).
- **Name pronunciation:** name Andrealphus, raspy, loudly, with PH sounding /f/.
- **Pantacular colours:** key-sigil in blue on orange background.
- **Basic colour:** orange.
- **Sound frequencies:** G music note (392 Hz) and C-sharp music note (554 Hz) sounding together.

CIMEIES

66

▲ Qliphotic Mercurian force in the mental and emotional levels of the neuropsyche, which is to be manifested and controlled; levels identified with the entity-code Cimeies.

- **Attainments:** capacity to learn grammar and languages; aggressive rhetorical skills; conflicting discursive impetus; ability to discover important hidden informations.
- **Qabalistic qlipha:** Samael – the "shell" of Mercurian forces; name pronounced clearly, hoarsely, and with a hissing S.
- **Operation hours:** 3rd and 10th night hours of Wednesday.
- **Psychoaromata:** storax (benzoin).
- **Name pronunciation:** name Cimeies, raspy, harshly.
- **Pantacular colours:** key-sigil in blue on orange background.
- **Basic colour:** orange.
- **Sound frequencies:** G music note (392 Hz) and C-sharp music note (554 Hz) sounding together.

67

▲ Qliphotic Solarian force in the mental and emotional levels of the neuropsyche, which is to be manifested and controlled; levels identified with the entity-code Amdusias.

- **Attainments:** capacity to be compliant, complacent, and flexible, and to demonstrate understanding; ability to convince, move and calm people, for specific purposes; ease of learning the musical arts.
- **Qabalistic qlipha:** Thagiriron – the "shell" of Solarian forces; name pronounced clearly, gutturally, and quickly.
- **Operation hours:** 3rd and 10th night hours of Sunday. (See *Appendix 1 – Hours table* and *Appendix 2 – Hours calculation*)
- **Psychoaromata:** spikenard.
- **Name pronunciation:** name Amdusias, raspy, clearly, with S sounding /ss/.
- **Pantacular colours:** key-sigil in violet on yellow background.
- **Basic colour:** yellow.
- **Sound frequencies:** E music note (330 Hz) and A-sharp music note (466 Hz) sounding together.

BELIAL

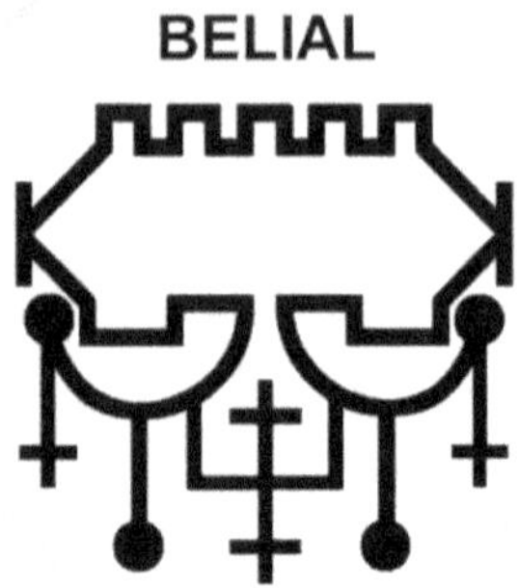

68

▲ Qliphotic Terrestrian force in the mental and emotional levels of the neuropsyche, which is to be manifested and controlled; levels identified with the entity-code Belial.

- **Attainments:** understanding of the rigid laws of the material world; courage, determination, and willingness to change things for bigger goals; capacity to break free from harmful greed and material world addictions; ability for persuasion and obtaining material favours from friends or enemies; ability to get social ascension; aptitude for flattery and adulation, aiming the personal interests; cunning and malice to mislead for material gain.
- **Qabalistic qlipha:** Lilith – the "shell" of Terrestrian forces; name pronounced deeply, slightly guttural, and slowly.
- **Operation hours:** 3rd and 10th night hours of Saturday.
- **Psychoaromata:** myrrh.
- **Name pronunciation:** name Belial, or Beliel, slightly guttural, clearly, pleasantly.
- **Pantacular colours:** key-sigil in purple, crimson, olive green, and white striped on ochre yellow, rust red, and black background.
- **Basic colour:** black.
- **Sound frequencies:** B music note (494 Hz) and F music note (699 Hz) sounding together.

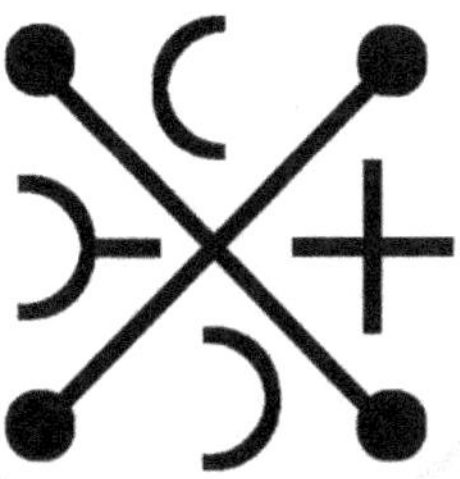

69

▲ Qliphotic Lunarian force in the mental and emotional levels of the neuropsyche, which is to be manifested and controlled; levels identified with the entity-code Decarabia.

- **Attainments:** ability to alter and expand the mind and keep control, for getting psychomental pleasure; capacity to learn natural sciences; poetic skills; capacity to tolerate people's unconscious and uncontrolled chatter, prattle, gabble, babble, and gibberish.
- **Qabalistic qlipha:** Gamaliel – the "shell" of Lunarian forces; name pronounced hoarsely, almost a whisper.
- **Operation hours:** 3rd and 10th night hours of Monday.
- **Psychoaromata:** wormwood.
- **Name pronunciation:** name Decarabia, almost a whisper, sustained, with oscillation in volume.
- **Pantacular colours:** key-sigil in yellow on violet background.
- **Basic colour:** violet.
- **Sound frequencies:** A music note (440 Hz) and D-sharp music note (622 Hz) sounding together.

<h1 style="text-align:center">SEIR</h1>

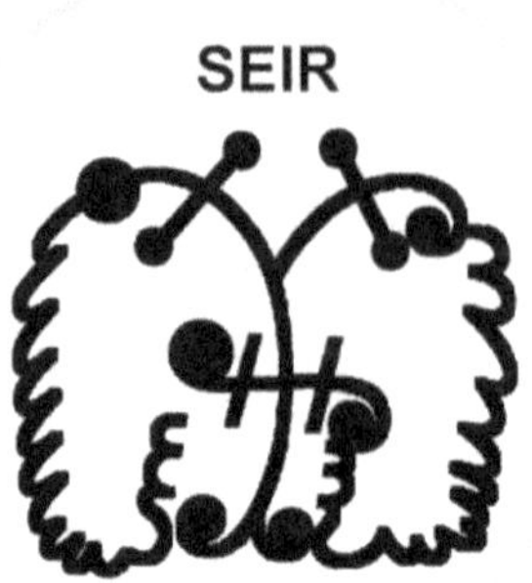

70

▲ Qliphotic Jupiterian force in the mental and emotional levels of the neuropsyche, which is to be manifested and controlled; levels identified with the entity-code Seir.

- **Attainments:** ability to gently extract true information from people, and to know about dishonest individuals and their victims; fraternal sense and willingness to share good things (material or not), wherever may be needed, or according to one's will; ability to perceive opportunities for earnings and growth; emotional intelligence to be in the right place at the right time; revelations that bring benefits; knowledge of things once hidden.
- **Qabalistic qlipha:** Gha'aseklah – the "shell" of Jupiterian forces; name pronounced clearly, deeply, strongly, with a sizzling S.
- **Operation hours:** 3rd and 10th night hours of Thursday.
- **Psychoaromata:** nutmeg.
- **Name pronunciation:** name Seir, or Seere, deep, clear, and strong, without aggressiveness.
- **Pantacular colours:** key-sigil in orange on blue background.
- **Basic colour:** blue.
- **Sound frequencies:** C music note (262 Hz) and F-sharp music note (370 Hz) sounding together.

DANTALION

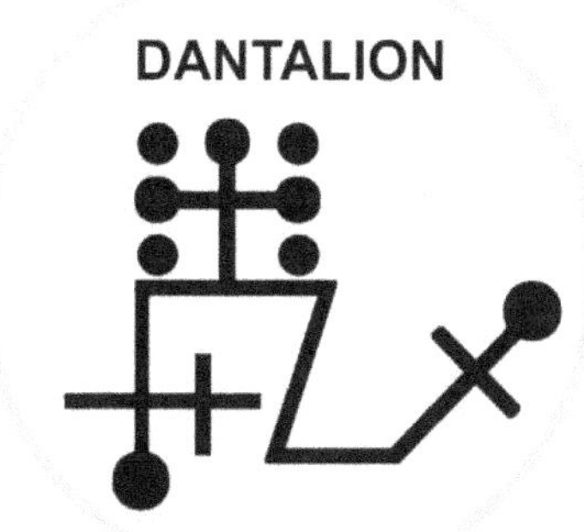

71

▲ Qliphotic Uranian force in the mental and emotional levels of the neuropsyche, which is to be manifested and controlled; levels identified with the entity-code Dantalion.

- **Attainments:** capacity to learn any sciences, arts, or philosophies, and teach to others; capacity to find specific useful information amidst the knowledge chaos; capacity to retrieve memories; ease of perceiving people's intentions; ability to emulate types of personalities, according to the situation or the objective; ability to persuasion, to change the way people think; seductive skills and attraction of people's interest.
- **Qabalistic qlipha:** Da'ath (also a sephira of the same name) – the "shell" of Uranian forces; name pronounced gutturally, and slowly.
- **Operation hours:** 1st night hour, at twilight, any day of the week. (See *Appendix 1 – Hours table* and *Appendix 2 – Hours calculation*)
- **Psychoaromata:** benzoin (1 part) and frankincense (1 part).
- **Name pronunciation:** name Dantalion, clearly.
- **Pantacular colours:** key-sigil in yellowish grey on purplish grey background.
- **Basic colour:** purplish grey.
- **Sound frequencies:** B-flat/A-sharp music note (466 Hz) and E music note (660 Hz) sounding together.

ANDROMALIUS

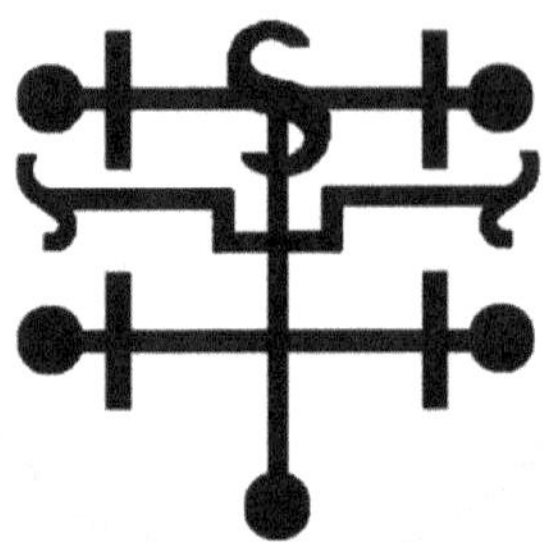

72

▲ Qliphotic Plutonian force in the mental and emotional levels of the neuropsyche, which is to be manifested and controlled; levels identified with the entity-code Andromalius.

- **Attainments:** ability to perceive the evil and malice of people; capacity to be confidence enough to deal with society at large; strength and courage to undertake fair compensations; capacity to be inflexible and cold--blooded to fight perverse, perfidious, and unrighteous people; ability to recover what has been "stolen" (concrete or abstract things); revelations; ability to obtain important knowledge.
- **Qabalistic qlipha:** Thaumiel – the "shell" of Plutonian forces; name pronounced clearly, strongly, gutturally, and quickly.
- **Operation hours:** 3rd and 10th night hours, any day of the week. (See *Appendix 1 – Hours table* and *Appendix 2 – Hours calculation*)
- **Psychoaromata:** camphor.
- **Name pronunciation:** name Andromalius, gutturally, strongly.
- **Pantacular colours:** key-sigil in black on white background.
- **Basic colour:** white.
- **Sound frequencies:** D music note (587 Hz) and G-sharp music note (831 Hz) sounding together.

IAO OPERATION

▲ Iao is the word or name whose vibration has the purpose of eliminating undesirable dispositions and moods and preparing the operator for the goetia operations described here. It is a code for the conscious neuropsyche higher function (the higher self, the individuality), which is beyond the prosaic and ordinary ego (the default mode neuropsyche).

1. Make four copies of the Iao seal in green on red background, 20 centimetre in diameter, and place each one on the wall (of the four quadrants or directions: west, south, east, and north), at the eye level, as you are standing.

2. Smoke the operations place using the incense burner or censer by burning a basic mixture composed of frankincense resin (1 part), myrrh (1 part), and benzoin (1 part) – or a natural incense that contains these elements. Start by smoking the west quadrant of the place and go south, east, and north, smoking the corners from bottom to top.

3. Light a red candle and place it on the centre of the bomos, and four black candles, one for each quadrant. The lamp on the ceiling must be on.

4. Sit down facing north quadrant and do polarized breathing (to facilitate mental concentration and generate a predisposition for goetic operations). Do this cycle 11 times:

- close the right nostril with the left-hand index finger and breath in through the left nostril;
- close the left nostril with the thumb and hold the breath for 11 seconds;
- open the right nostril and breath out;
- hold the breath for 11 seconds;
- breath in through the right nostril, close the right nostril with the index finger, and hold the breath for 11 seconds;
- open the left nostril, breath out, hold for 11 seconds, and restart breathing in through the same nostril.

5. Stand up, face north, breath in and visualize a luminous sphere of red energy in your navel area. Breath out visualizing the sphere expanding until it encompasses your entire body. Breath in and breath out 11 times, visualizing the red luminous sphere growing and enveloping the entire place.

6. Still facing north, perform the ceremonial bow (left palm covering right fist, at throat level, the arms horizontally).

7. Breath in and raise your arms to 90 degrees angle to the torso, and forearms bent 90 degrees to the arms. Visualize and feel yourself as a dragon with wings outstretched. Breath out.

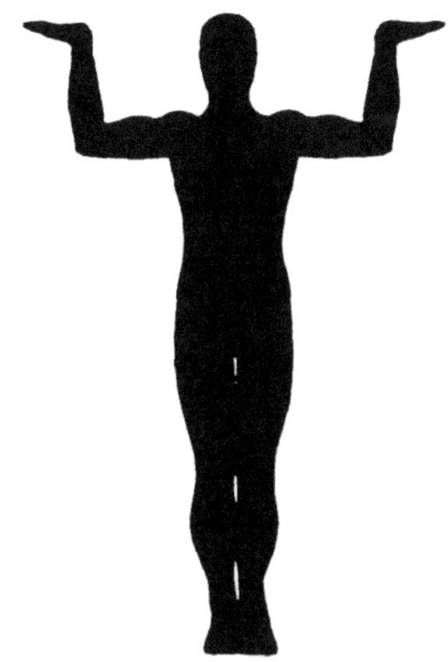

8. Breath in and breath out. At the same time, clap your hands at the level of your navel area and visualize the sphere of red energy chaotically blasting in luminous lightnings in all directions.

9. To create a neuropsychic force vortex, start in the west quadrant and face south, east, and north, like this:
- starting in the west quadrant, in a standing position with the right arm fully extended and straight beside the body, and the left arm and index finger pointing at the seal on the wall, concentrate on the seal, visualizing red energy coming out of finger and heading to the seal. Breath in and breath out, vibrating the name Iao in a whisper, slowly, pausing briefly after vibrating the letter O, then starting again, 3 times;
- with the left arm still pointing at the wall (seal), now face south, visualizing the red energy heading to the south quadrant seal. Vibrate the name Iao, suddenly, and choppy in each letter, for 3 times;
- now facing east, do the same, but vibrate the name softly, clearly, sustaining the sound of each letter, 3 times;
- now facing north, the same again, but vibrate the name in a dragged sound, aggressive, and guttural like a roar, 2 times.

10. Still facing north quadrant, sit down, be silent for as long as it feels necessary, in a relaxed way, concentrating on the seal with eyes open and then closed, assimilating the neuropsychic processes and being receptive to any knowledge insight.

11. Open your eyes, stand up, and perform the ceremonial bow (left palm covering right fist, at throat level, the arms horizontally), concentrating on the seal, thus ending this operation.

GOETIA OPERATION
(Active practice)

1. Take a shower. Optionally, make the anointing with the appropriate oil (see item "Psychoaromatas", p. 12). Wear the robe.

2. Draw a circle on the ground with chalk and sea salt, and place the bomos (or a suitable table or counter) in the centre, facing north. Outside, facing north, with at least 60 centimetres beyond the circle, place the goetic triangle. In this, in the centre, place the goetic key-sigil (in the appropriate pantacular colours) and the censer burning the appropriate psychoaromata, and, in the upper vertex of the triangle, put a candle in the appropriate basic colour.

3. Above the bomos, on the ceiling, a soft white light lamp. On the bomos, place:
   - north quadrant, a candlestick with a candle in the appropriate basic colour, optionally anointed with the appropriate essential oil;
   - centre, another key-sigil in the appropriate colours;
   - east quadrant, another censer with appropriate incense;
   - south quadrant, the wand, horizontally;
   - west quadrant, the hand bell.

4. Smoke the place with the appropriate psychoaromata.

5. Perform the Iao Operation (p. 89).

6. Visualize the place, the bomos, and the triangle, breathing 11 times.

7. Ring the bell 11 times, with an interval, like this: ❘ ❘❘❘❘❘❘❘❘❘❘

8. Facing north, at the bomos, in a standing position, legs together, spine straight and erect, raise your arms to 90 degrees angle to the torso, and forearms bent 90 degrees to the arms. Do the self-exaltation:

> ***Ho Drakon Ho Archaios!***
> ***I, [name], exalt myself as Logos and Antilogos!***
> ***And I call the Dragon to be with me in my***
> ***attainments by means of reason, will, and mastery,***
> ***and take me to the levels of Knowledge!***
> ***Ho Drakon Ho Archaios!***

9. Ring the bell 11 times, like this: ❘❘❘❘❘❘❘❘❘❘❘

10. Focus on your attainment (goal, objective, problem to be solved, etc.), clearly, no hesitation, no confusion, and no ambiguities.

11. Concentrate on the goetic key-sigil, taking 11 deep breaths.

12. Take the wand in your left hand and point it at the key-sigil in the triangle.

13. Focus on your attainment, raise your emotions (but under control), take a deep breath, and say 11 times:

> ***I, [name], now access the powers of [goetic entity name],***
> ***which transit between the levels, for the accomplishment***
> ***of my will!***

14. Still in self-exaltation, and pointing the wand at the triangle, repeat the name of the goetic entity-code 11 times, or until you feel it is enough.

15. If the goetic manifestation is not yet perceived, take the key-
-sigil that is on the bomos and bring it close to the candle fire:

*I, [name], **in possession of reason, will, and mastery,
I want to access the powers of** [goetic entity name]**!
That I gain access, or be disintegrated
the name and symbol of** [goetic entity name]**!***

*That the manifestation of** [goetic entity name]
**may be intelligible!
Under the powers of** [appropriate qlipha name]
and under my authority!*

16. If the goetic manifestation is perceived, authoritatively declare
the objectives to be accomplished, clearly and specifically, without
hesitation:

*I, [name], **want the powers of** [goetic entity name]**!
May** [goetic entity name] **carry out my demands,**
[here, you say the demands, attainments, etc.]**,
without any prejudice!***

17. Still pointing the wand at the goetic key-sigil in the triangle,
take a deep breath and say:

*I, [name], **having my will fulfilled,
I return** [goetic entity name]
**to your own and original levels, so that you wait
and always be available for my demands!***

18. Still facing north, at the bomos, in a standing position, legs
together, spine straight and erect, raise your arms to 90 degrees
angle to the torso, and forearms bent 90 degrees to the arms. Do
the self-exaltation:

*Ho Drakon Ho Archaios!
I, [name], exalt myself as Logos and Antilogos!
And I integrate myself into the Dragon
That took me to the levels of Knowledge!
Ho Drakon Ho Archaios!*

19. Ring the bell 11 times, with an interval, like this: |||||||||| |

20. Keep the key-sigil in an envelope identified by goetic entity name.

21. Perform the Iao Operation (p. 89).

22. Take off your robe, put everything away, and go distract your-self with other things.

GOETIA OPERATION
(Semi-passive practice)

1. Take a shower. Optionally, make the anointing with the appropriate oil (see item "Psychoaromatas", p. 12). Wear the robe.

2. Draw a circle on the ground with chalk and sea salt, and place a chair, facing north, in the centre. On the left side of the chair, place a small table with the hand bell, the wand, and, optionally, a sound device prepared to play the appropriate frequencies. Outside the circle, in front of the chair, with at least 60 centimetres beyond the circle, place the bomos (or a suitable table or counter). On the side of the bomos facing the chair, at the eye level, as you are standing, attach the goetic triangle with the key-sigil (in the appropriate pantacular colours). On top of the bomos, place a candle in the appropriate basic colour; on the floor, leaning against the bomos, place the censer burning the appropriate psychoaromata. If there is no bomos or counter, attach the goetic triangle on the wall in front

of you, placing the candle and censer on the floor below the triangle. On the ceiling, a soft white light lamp.

3. Smoke the place with the appropriate psychoaromata.

4. Perform the Iao Operation (p. 89).

5. Visualize the place and the triangle, breathing 11 times.

6. Ring the bell 11 times, with an interval, like this: | |||||||||||

7. Facing the triangle, in a standing position, legs together, spine straight and erect, raise your arms to 90 degrees angle to the torso, and forearms bent 90 degrees to the arms. Do the self-exaltation:

> *Ho Drakon Ho Archaios!*
> *I, [name], exalt myself as Logos and Antilogos!*
> *And I call the Dragon to be with me in my*
> *attainments by means of reason, will, and mastery,*
> *and take me to the levels of Knowledge!*
> *Ho Drakon Ho Archaios!*

8. Sit on the chair and ring the bell 11 times, like this: |||||||||||

9. Focus on your attainment (goal, objective, problem to be solved, etc.), clearly, no hesitation, no confusion, and no ambiguities.

10. Concentrate on the goetic key-sigil, taking 11 deep breaths.

11. Take the wand in your left hand and point it at the key-sigil in the triangle.

12. Focus on your attainment, raise your emotions (but under control), take a deep breath, and say 11 times:

> *I, [name], now access the powers of [goetic entity name], which transit between the levels, for the accomplishment of my will!*
>
> *That the manifestation of [goetic entity name] may be intelligible! Under the powers of [appropriate qlipha name] and under my authority!*

13. If the goetic manifestation is perceived, authoritatively declare the objectives to be accomplished, clearly and specifically, without hesitation:

> *I, [name], want the powers of [goetic entity name]! May [goetic entity name] carry out my demands, [here, you say the demands, attainments, etc.], without any prejudice!*

14. Place the wand on the small table and concentrate on the triangle, repeating the name of the goetic entity-code 11 times, or until you feel it is enough.

15. Optionally, turn on the device to play the sound frequencies of the goetic entity-code.

16. Close your eyes, take 11 deep breaths, and aim for the goetic experience, which may include knowledge acquisition, attainments anticipation, sudden and useful thoughts, feelings, visions.

17. As you feel it is enough, take the wand and point it at the goetic key-sigil in the triangle. Take a deep breath, and say:

***I, [name], having my will fulfilled,**
I return [goetic entity name]
**to your own and original levels, so that you wait
and always be available for my demands!***

18. Ring the bell 11 times, like this: ||||||||||||

19. Stand up, in a standing position, legs together, spine straight and erect, raise your arms to 90 degrees angle to the torso, and forearms bent 90 degrees to the arms. Do the self-exaltation:

***Ho Drakon Ho Archaios!**
I, [name], exalt myself as Logos and Antilogos!
And I integrate myself into the Dragon
That took me to the levels of Knowledge!
Ho Drakon Ho Archaios!*

20. Ring the bell 11 times, with an interval, like this: |||||||||| |

21. Keep the key-sigil in an envelope identified by goetic entity name.

22. Perform the Iao Operation (p. 89).

23. Take off your robe, put everything away, and go distract yourself with other things.

Appendix 1

Hours table

Night hours

The night hours begin with sunset

Night hour	Sunday	Monday	Tuesday	Wednesday	Thursday	Friday	Saturday	Saturday
1st	Uranus	Uranus	Uranus	Uranus	Uranus	Uranus	*Uranus*	
1st	Jupiter/Neptune	Venus	Saturn	Sun	Moon	Mars/Pluto	Mercury	Earth
2nd	Mars/Pluto	Mercury	Jupiter/Neptune	Venus	Saturn	Sun	Moon	Earth
3rd	*Sun*	*Moon*	*Mars/Pluto*	*Mercury*	*Jupiter/Neptune*	*Venus*	*Saturn*	Earth
4th	Venus	Saturn	Sun	Moon	Mars/Pluto	Mercury	Jupiter/Neptune	Earth
5th	Mercury	Jupiter/Neptune	Venus	Saturn	Sun	Moon	Mars/Pluto	Earth
6th	Moon	Mars/Pluto	Mercury	Jupiter/Neptune	Venus	Saturn	Sun	Earth
7th	Saturn	Sun	Moon	Mars/Pluto	Mercury	Jupiter/Neptune	Venus	Earth
8th	Jupiter/Neptune	Venus	Saturn	Sun	Moon	Mars/Pluto	Mercury	Earth
9th	Mars/Pluto	Mercury	Jupiter/Neptune	Venus	Saturn	Sun	Moon	Earth
10th	*Sun*	*Moon*	*Mars/Pluto*	*Mercury*	*Jupiter/Neptune*	*Venus*	*Saturn*	Earth
11th	Venus	Saturn	Sun	Moon	Mars/Pluto	Mercury	Jupiter/Neptune	Earth
12th	Mercury	Jupiter/Neptune	Venus	Saturn	Sun	Moon	Mars/Pluto	Earth

Appendix 2

Hours calculation

Calculation of night hours (example)

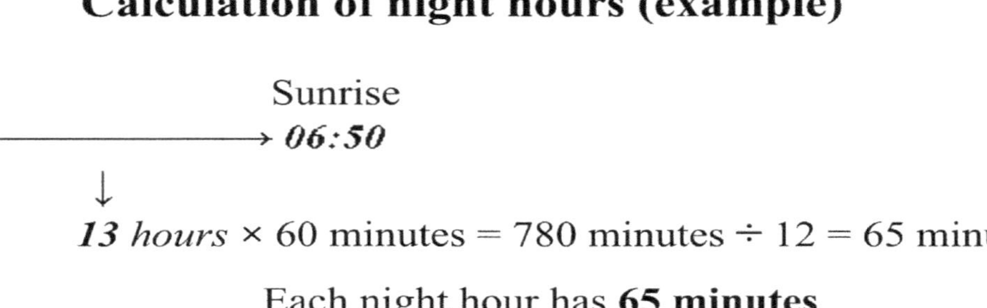

Appendix 3
Glossary

Astralization – Act or effect of astralizing, which is to charge goals, desires, and images with emotional-intellective energy.

Attainment – Act or effect of attaining or achieving; to carry out operational processes, obtaining specific results.

Ego – Totality of neural activities of the superficial neuropsyche system, the default mode network, which is the source of human suffering; default system that works without the conscious control of the individual (who is overloaded with thinkings, personal reflections and self-reflections, which is usually damaging in some way).

Knowledge, Tree of – Qabalistic diagrammatic representation of the elevenian system of information in the "nocturnal aspect", with the qliphotic spheres ("shells") and the setian tunnels; diagram that represents the neuropsychic system and the physical constitution of the human being and the universe.

Liberal arts and sciences – Concept from Ancient Times (5th century) and Middle Ages. It refers to a set of subjects called *quadrivium* (arithmetic, geometry, astronomy, music) and *trivium* (grammar, logic, rhetoric).

Pantacle – Round "plate" (pantacular plate) made of rigid material (paper, wood), and it is, by neuropsychic convention, an active and dynamic tool that represents the whole, in physical form, of a specific force (from the Greek word *panto* = "whole", "all", "everything") and in which symbols, keys-sigils, words, and pertinent numbers are inserted, in the appropriate colours, serving for defined functions and objectives and activating a certain neuropsychic aspect in the individual; pantacle is different from pentacle – this being the symbol of the pentagram, the five--pointed star (from the Greek word *penta* = "five"), inside the circle.

Psychoaromata – Aromatic substance that can affect the neuropsyche, influencing the emotions and thoughts.

Psychomental – Emotion and reason as a unit.

Qlipha (in the plural: qliphoth) – "Shell"; each of the eleven qabalistic spheres of the Tree of Knowledge (the diagram of the elevenian system), to which sidereal objects and many other correspondences are assigned; the "nightside" of existence, the darkness where wisdom is hidden (the deep levels of the neuropsyche).

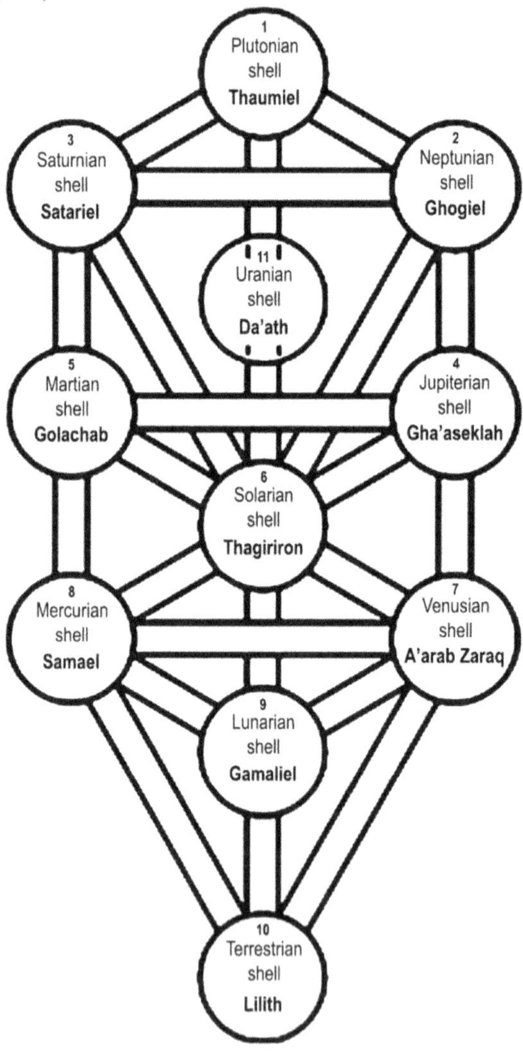

Bibliography

BETZ, H.D. (ed.). *The greek magical papyri in translation*. Chicago: University of Chicago, 1986.

MONT, A.C. *A cabala draconiana*. São Paulo: Sitra Ahra Editora, 2020.

MONT, A.C. *Sistemagia*: o grimório eleveniano. São Paulo: Sitra Ahra Editora, 2022.

WHITE, N. (ed.). *Lemegeton*: the goetia. Exact photocopy of the 17th Century Manuscript from the British Museum (Sloane 2731). El Sobrante, CA: The Technology Group, 1994.

A.C. Mont

A.C. Mont is a writer and artist. He published the works *Sistemagia – O Grimório Eleveniano*, *A Cabala Draconiana*, *Liber Luciferi*, and others. He was a member of semi-secret and discrete societies such as Ordo Draconis, Freemasonry, and Mensa Society.

In addition to his work, A.C. Mont: has illustrations and essays published in Poland, in the book *The Way of the Serpent* (Magan Publications); has poetry published in England, in the book *Mandragora* (Scarlet Imprint); has articles published in the music journal *Roadie Crew*; was a contributor to the journal *Universo Maçônico*; was a contributor to the journal *Lucifer Luciferax*; was a contributor to the websites Morte Súbita, Teoria da Conspiração, and Whiplash; has excerpts from his writings published in academic materials, such as the journal *Estação Literária* (v.12, Jan. 2014) and the book *As Malasartes de Lúcifer* (2012), on philosophy and literature, both from the State University of Londrina; has participated in the program Arquétipos broadcast by Rádio Mundial (São Paulo, Brazil); has participated in the program Vox Vampyrica broadcast by Rádio Antena Zero (São Paulo, Brazil); has participated in a documentary series for TV Brasil; has participated as a lecturer at the Simpósio de Hermetismo, in São Paulo; was a collaborating artist at *Zupi*, a trilingual art and graphic design magazine; is the editor and creator of the journal *Sitra Ahra*, which has the participation of international authors; is the creator and performer of the music project Qliphotica.